Halfway

A Memoir

Tom Macher

SCRIBNER

New York   London   Toronto   Sydney   New Delhi

Scribner
An Imprint of Simon & Schuster, Inc.
1230 Avenue of the Americas
New York, NY 10020

First Scribner hardcover edition February 2018

SCRIBNER and design are registered trademarks of The Gale Group, Inc.,
used under license by Simon & Schuster, Inc., the publisher of this work.

For information about special discounts for bulk purchases,
please contact Simon & Schuster Special Sales at 1-866-506-1949
or business@simonandschuster.com.

The Simon & Schuster Speakers Bureau can bring authors to your live event.
For more information or to book an event contact the Simon & Schuster Speakers
Bureau at 1-866-248-3049 or visit our website at www.simonspeakers.com.

Interior design by Kyle Kabel

Manufactured in the United States of America

1   3   5   7   9   10   8   6   4   2

Library of Congress Control Number: 2017049581

ISBN 978-1-5011-1260-7
ISBN 978-1-5011-1264-5 (ebook)

For my family,
and the people I knew and loved when I was younger;
I wish I could tell the story better.

Contents

Contents

Halfway

Prologue

WE were never alone in the House. That's the first thing. Never. There was always some brother around, if not a few, like on the back slab, or front porch, or they were about to come running, someone was, some guy, wanting to talk. Talking meant group. We were always in group. Even our daily things. Like we didn't eat dinner; we went to Dinner Group. And, afterward, we didn't clean; we performed Kitchen Clean-up Group. Having a feeling? Want to confront someone? You called group. We were always confronting someone. Half the time, we barely made it to the Coke machine before another group got called. Showering felt off, using the bathroom, getting dressed. All of it strange, like you were doing something wrong, and you had to be quick about it, like any moment someone would burst through the door, calling group. The second thing is, we cleaned a lot. All the time. But at least cleaning, like down-on-your-knees cleaning, like wiping the base of a toilet, you were alone. Twice, maybe three times, I found myself being the only brother on Property. That's it. Middle of the afternoon, too. The first time, I didn't even think about it, just went straight to my room, lay down in bed,

1

and played with myself. Every Sunday, Tuesday, and Thursday night we had scheduled groups. Scheduled meant Staff had prepared, which meant watch out. They were events. Dudes showered before them. They brushed their teeth. We could not miss these groups for anything. Not work, not sickness, not a near-death experience. Miss one and that's it, your ass is gone. And what about the store? Or watching TV? Or shooting hoops? Most of the time, we could only do these things if we were in group. Like on Flats or Stricts, everything was done in group. Now, we weren't even alone when we showered. There'd be ten guys outside the bathroom door. And try to beat off in that environment. Try rubbing one out with ten dudes moaning and slapping their cheeks. I promise you this: it got done. Anything, short of using, was okay, *if* we did it in group. And when something went wrong, as something often did, say someone stole something, or shot crystal, or banged a girl, or had admitted knowing of some other brother who had, but didn't want to rat, we had Standing Honesty Group, where we couldn't sit, talk, or move until that dude ratted or someone else fessed up. Didn't matter he didn't want to talk. We stood in silence until he either spoke or walked. Sometimes Staff came in during these groups carrying the vials, and we'd wait until our names got called. Once our names got called, we peed. Then dudes for sure left. Even before the results came back. But some guys who pissed dirty stayed. These dudes said amazing things when Staff showed them their labs. Hell, no; it was poppy seeds, or they got roofied, or rolled, or drank spiked ice tea, a damn needle fell from the sky. Or they appealed to our humanity. Their mom died. Their baby got sick. They offered convoluted tales starring their shitty job, dickhead boss, the damn heat, the endless rain, the humidity, a flat tire on their bike, or the motherfucker of a freight train that held them up on the wrong side of the tracks, you get the idea. It didn't take long to hear it all. Mostly, we clutched our nuts. Or laughed. Straight laughed. In their face. Complete with joking groans: Poor me, poor me, pour me another drink! Not because nothing fazed us, just we'd gotten used to it, that's all. And besides, it *was* funny—we could relate to the thinking behind it, how we'll convince ourselves any idea is a good one. But sometimes a guy couldn't pee. He was nervous or dehydrated or just pissed like, what, five minutes ago. Then we waited. We stayed in that room until everyone peed. Other guys refused to pee. If we refused to pee, we were gone. Still, dudes wouldn't. It didn't matter if they were facing hard time, didn't matter the House was the only thing keeping them alive, they wouldn't pee. Once, a guy pissed himself, waiting. He wore yellow gym shorts, a pair of scuffed Air Maxes, no socks. The pee darkened his shorts, bounced off his knee, and pooled on the Group Room floor. We laughed, of course, but it wasn't funny—he'd smoked rock and was going to get kicked out and we'd have to clean this mess up.

I must've seen a thousand guys pass through, many of them headed for worse places, and much worse things, but each of them feels the same to mc now, as if they are all some version of myself that I'll never fully come to terms with. I miss them.

Unripe Fruit

Long before any of this, and before I was born, even, my mom had a baby named Aidan. She was married then. And she and her husband, a flimflam type, moved from Philly to rural New York to start a commune called the Farm of the Message. A guru ran the place, a man who wore a white beard and white robes. He taught meditations unifying various religious philosophies under the guiding principles of beauty, harmony, and love. It was New Age. And they were believers. But shortly after having another boy, Lee—sweet Lee, born bowlegged, pigeon-toed, and knock-kneed—old Flimflam moved on, filed for divorce, and demanded full custody of both children. The guru presided. He said Flimflam could only get one. As a result, we rarely saw Aidan growing up, once a year at most, and when my mom met a man and got pregnant with me, she promised herself no one would take me away.

She was thirty-two, prematurely gray. She wore glasses, corduroys, maternity clothes. Consumed by sadness and pestered by doubt, she questioned herself—what kind of mother loses a child? Here was Lee, his legs broken to correct his condition, all plaster-casted and braced but happy, and here were her finances—zero—and soon another one—what the hell was she thinking? She didn't even know my father, not really; never would. He'd arrived on the commune in a VW after driving cross-country, popping black beauties and dropping LSD, losing his mind in Nebraska, Indiana, Ohio, he and some others, all of them hopeful. On the commune they found hard work, a lot of it, and not much else. He didn't know about me when he split for San Francisco, figured that was that, he'd never hear word of it again. He got a job, began living. Seven months later, my mom showed up with Lee and a very large belly, her smile half happy, half apology; whatever my parents tried together that fall did not go well.

She didn't even tell him our destination, just bounced. Brought us crosstown to the Avenues. This part of the city was once all sand dunes, but had long ago been developed. Rows of Victorians stretched to the ocean. Hilly, windswept, and covered in a layer of marine fog so thick there's never sunshine, it exists in perpetual grays, which seems right somehow. That morning, she held me in her arms and pulled Lee's carriage, marching through torrents of rain, determined, defiant, a single mother. Finally, we came to a Victorian cloaked by the weather. This is our new home, my mom said. It's where we'll live. Things will be good here.

It was not our home, of course, but someone else's—a friend's—as my mom was broke and, with the two young kids, unemployable. A few months later, we got on an airplane, and once more she explained the ramifications. We're leaving here, she said, not coming back. Not any time soon, anyway. She lifted me above her head so that my arms flapped out,

as if in flight. Don't worry, she said. Don't worry. No one will
ever take you away.

SHE HAD NO FAMILY, no home. Her only place of refuge
was the commune, and she dreaded going back there. So we
moved a lot, subsisting on the grace of others, sleeping on
couches in living rooms, in spare beds, and on blankets piled
high on hardwood floors, each place buying her more time
where she didn't have to decide, as if she had another option,
as if something else might arise—a better plan, new hope—as
if all this moving wasn't leading us back to the commune, but
by June 1978 we were living in a cramped second-floor room
in a dilapidated Shaker dormitory and taking our meals in a
communal dining hall at the Farm of the Message.

It spanned hundreds of acres, all of it rustic, wooded, or
fully arable; in its creaky buildings were cellars and staircases,
places to hide. A lot of families lived in these dorms, each with
many kids. It was, it seemed, *kind of* the perfect place to raise
children. I remember being happy there. Lee, too. Photos
capture his arm around my shoulder; he wears a beret, I have
a hammer; we're both grinning. In other pictures we pose on
tractors, again smiling, or stand half-naked in sunflowers and
on gravel roads, or drape from each other on cracked stoops,
thrilled with the world and each other, shirtless, covered in
mud or bare-assed, our essentials exposed, damn near always
swimming, tottering in pumpkin patches, investigating stacks
of wood or an old pickup. Lee had black curls and I was tow-
headed, angelic: cowlicks rose winglike behind my ears. The

difference felt important: my locks implied lightness, but only in these photos with Lee did I express any levity. The rest of the time I brooded, my eyes these dark orbs full of suspicion and doubt. Whatever plagues me now, I know I had then, too.

LEE'S LEGS HEALED. Now, if you didn't watch him, he might pee in a potted plant or a trash can. Mom had communal responsibilities—she was on the welcoming committee and helped deliver babies—and meditations to practice and matters of the heart that required her attention, and she was not around much those days. So Lee and I would just get up and go. I recall a vague curiosity about nearly everything. In the woods or graveyard, in the root cellar or hayloft, in the greenhouse or the old chair factory, we'd come across an adult who'd pick us up in their arms, or hold us in their lap as they tractored the field. We had quite a few sitters, most of them nice people. They'd set us down in a row of strawberries where we'd dream. These were my favorite moments, coming to in a plot of fruit, sun rays warming my skin, Lee dozing next to me.

One lady used to pull my arms through the banister and duct-tape my wrists. Let's play prisoner, she'd say. Then she'd disappear. I don't know what happened after, where she'd go. Places of spiritual growth attract all types, and indeed among these idealists was the knowhow to start a birthing center, an organic farm, a bakery, an herb garden, a VW repair shop, a school, and yet, except for the auto shop, none of these businesses made money, and all these dreamers brought their own demons and doubts, their own pasts and inner lives, and despite how much any of us wants something better, the truth is we rarely get far from ourselves, no matter how many miles we travel.

I've had to learn this myself many, many times now.

TELL YOU A HAPPY STORY. We moved out of our room in the Shaker building and down a gravel road past the commune farm and a pond to a cabin deep in the woods. I was three, Lee five, and all summer, as we tramped back and forth along this gravel road, he promised we'd creep onto the farm one of these days and steal all the strawberries. In August, he said, once they ripen. And sure enough, one morning we woke before the sun and walked up that road to where the trees broke and descended upon the farm as if locusts. We ate every strawberry in that field. Row after row. We ate all of them. Until they were gone. It was dark when we began but light now. Chins sticky, fingers pink. I thought, Well, this has been quite nice indeed, we set out to accomplish something, and now that it's done we will go, but Lee wanted to eat the green ones, too. Don't do it, I warned him. You're crazy. But he couldn't help himself. He laughed and laughed. It was funny. He ate all the unripe fruit he could, strawberries so hard and tart his eyes crossed into themselves and he grew dizzy and had to sit down. He rolled onto his face and retched. Oh, he said. Oh.

Also, our mom got married again.

A Bastard in the Family

WE moved again. This time to Brooklyn, which wasn't farmers' markets and fancy boutiques back then. Instead we found dirty snow, barred windows, double and triple locks, soot, sirens, domestic disputes; breaking and entering seemed popular. Cars, or so my mom said, backfired regularly.

I used to walk to the sidewalk a lot, and then turn back to our apartment.

We were poor, we struggled. A claustrophobic feeling menaced our lives. This is the misery of the broke: leaving the apartment meant spending money. We had a car, but it never worked. We had lights, but they fluttered, dimmed, and burned out. We used to watch our mom's husband tinker under the station wagon's hood, slink from the hood to the driver's seat, crank the ignition, try it again, shake his head. While grocery shopping, our mom practiced simple addition, held up the line, removed items from her basket, performed sleight of hand, the five-finger discount.

One day I found her on the bedroom floor, an empty bowl on the hardwood, pennies spilled everywhere, maybe a dollar total. She counted carefully, sliding each penny into one of two separate piles. She was crying.

I asked was she hurt. No, she said, removing her glasses and wiping her wet brown eyes. But her shoulders bobbed, the tears kept coming.

But you're crying, I said.

That doesn't mean I'm hurt.

Well, if you are, I said, you should tell me.

I'm just sad, she said.

Why?

I want to be able to afford to buy you things, she said. I don't care what. Just something. A snack, a toy, ice cream. Anything.

My heart shattered in my chest, tore open. I don't want anything, I said.

It's not the thing, she said, her voice breaking with despair, but the ability.

WE HAD NO IDEA what to call her new husband. His birth name got bandied about. As did "Dad." Yet Lee and I hardly knew what "Dad" meant. We settled on a loose Hebrew translation, a term of endearment like "Pop" or "Daddy," Abba. And for his part, Abba fit the bill. Despite our family's weird construction—our halves and lacks, the unknowing—he was determined to make it in New York City as a provider. Every day he put on a suit and tie and set out to find work in Manhattan and every night came back wearing overalls, his beard and curly hair spattered with paint. He worked hard, was athletic, distant, motivated. On the weekends he played softball, brought us along, and introduced us to such finery as the chili dog, Coney Island, and Far Rockaway Beach. We kept mice in a box, took them to Long Island or the park when the car quit working again. Finally, we got a new car, but it seemed the same—another barely operational station wagon that sputtered to life and died again. Aidan visited. Then he left. My mom was crying. I could go on; I could stab you a thousand times with sadness. These weren't good years. They were full of little anxious nothings and long silences.

Mom, I'd say, but she'd just look at me, her eyes always on the verge.

She was tall, five foot eight, and extremely nearsighted, almost myopic, and she told me these things of herself—the early gray, the height and poor vision—would be passed on to me as they had been passed on to her by her family through genetics, which worried me. She had no family beyond us. Her mom died when she was young. Her dad was dead. She had a brother, but he disappeared after the war. Not a POW, not MIA or AWOL, he just never came back. There was no one else. No aunts, uncles, grandparents, or cousins. She had no one. I, too, felt as if I had no one beyond them. Everywhere I turned, every question just led to more lack: Who is my dad? What's he like? What happened with you and him? Did y'all love each other? Will I know him? Will I ever meet my family? And what about Aidan? What's his deal? Will he ever live with us?

I tried to make her feel better.

I wish I could meet your family, I told her once.

She knelt and kissed my forehead. I'm so glad, she said, you never will.

*   *   *

LEE AND I were playing on the sidewalk. I believe he had a broom in his hand, and I had a spatula, and we were thwacking each other about the neck, head, and face. I'm not sure if the reality of our different fathers had set in yet or if we'd fully transitioned from happy children to the monsters we'd become, or if this game of beating each other had already become our favorite, as it one day would, but I know it's what we were doing when a taxi appeared at our curb. The oldest person I'd ever seen hopped out.

I turned and ran for our flat, but my mom appeared in the doorway, drying soapy hands on her apron. She likes to clean when she's nervous.

Here he is, the old man said. Let's have a look, shall we? He turned me by my waist. An equally old woman teetered in the taxi's backseat, a crooked grin on her face—they'd been drinking. Come on, the old man said. Hop in. He waved at my mom. We'll have him back soon enough. I promise.

I'm not getting in that cab, I said. Not with you. No way.

Sweetie, my mom said. This man is your grampa.

Abba's dad?

No, she said. Your *dad's* dad.

Huh. C'mon, Lee, I said. This was interesting to me. Let's see what he wants.

No, my mom said. Lee's staying. Now go on. I'm through arguing about this.

They took me to FAO Schwarz, where this tall man jumped out from an aisle, waving his hands as if he were a magician. Hell-o, he said. Hell-o!

Who are you? I asked.

I own this place, he informed me. He pulled toys from the

shelves and handed them to me—spaceships, soldiers, robots, mechanical spiders. A lot of stuff. I suddenly missed my brother.

I turned to my grampa. Seriously, I said. Who's this dude? He my father?

Father's brother, my grampa said, which was pretty cool. This guy was fun.

My father's brother owned a penthouse overlooking Central Park. We arrived to find many people swilling about, laughing and carrying on. They twirled in their fine haberdashery, chasing highballs with bumps of cocaine. They were having a party.

My uncle handed me money, a lot of it. From my pocket, he produced a twenty, found another behind my ear. Other adults gathered about, touching my hair and pulling my cheeks, all of them offering cash dollars. I felt very far from our poverty in Brooklyn.

The crowd surged, buckled, and then ebbed, swept me off my feet. I landed in front of a couch where a bald man was sitting. He wore a playboy's mustache, aviator shades. Martini in hand, he'd been explaining things to someone next to him. A cigarette dangled from the frozen smile on his face.

He seemed surprised and said something, a small joke, I don't know what. No one laughed. He was still smiling, but the smile felt mean. This wasn't a happy man, I knew. He held me for a moment before handing me back to my grampa. Then he stood, patted his pockets, and left.

First memory of my dad.

That Piece of Shit Your Father

SCHOOL started, which I'd been looking forward to. I wanted friends. We didn't have any, Lee and I. No one in our neighborhood seemed to like us much. They said we were different. And not just our hair or skin color but what we talked about. A farm, they'd say, really? A farm? And Lee, they said, you fag. That's a last name.

But getting on the bus, I found more of the same. Look at this here, the other children said. A couple strangers. Come here with that white-ass hair. Let me touch it.

I got angry, said things kids say—fuck you, I'll kill you—full of stink-eye, waving my fists, but Lee turned inward, sad, aloof.

In the quiet of our apartment, he pulled me aside. These boys are mean, he said. And you're going to have to learn to turn the other cheek. You can always go in the other room, he said. It doesn't make you weak. You can just ignore them. You don't have to listen, don't have to say anything. You can just curl up in a ball, if you have to, and disappear.

No longer happy, Lee had trouble sleeping. He'd sleepwalk or get terrors. We'd find him in REM on the counter or stoop, on the curb or street. He told me awful, uncommon things when I found him staring out our window, watching the alley. He was waiting for a man, he claimed, who raped a woman out there the night before with a screwdriver. He was six years old.

One day in school I was looking at a book with pictures of horses. This wasn't cool, the other kids said, but strange, man on man, sissy, for girls.

I remembered Lee's warning and brought the book across the room, drew my head in, but they kept after it. Oh, that horse, they said, with its fat ding-a-ling. One of them got in my ear. Hey, horse-fucker, he said. I'm talking to you. He slammed the book on my nose. I started bleeding. There was a lot of blood, actually.

Then more blood. I grabbed the boy's arm in my hands and bit into his biceps as you might a pork rib.

That night or maybe the next, my mom and Abba called Lee and me into their bedroom, told us to pack our things, we were moving again, to Atlanta, which was far away, and warm.

What about my dad? I asked. How will he find me there?

Oh, sweetie, my mom said. Or something like that.

THEY SAY AFTER A WHILE a train's rumble is white noise and you stop hearing it, but I never did. Every hour that thing came, rattling our windows and doors. Even now I listen for that train. It was sort of an idyllic time. In Atlanta, our backyard bordered a park. Nearby was a high school, a college; there were woods and creeks, many bridges to drop things from and culverts to crawl through. There were snakes everywhere. We'd find them in the shed or under the porch and in the street after it rained, writhing about. Nearly every afternoon Abba took us to the park to play baseball. He was a lefty, slick with a glove, could throw a curveball, a slider, a knuckleball. Nothing had ever felt so good as swinging a bat, hitting a ball. Photos from Halloween feature Lee as Superman; I'm Chewbacca. When we weren't playing ball, we spent time on the railroad tracks. If a train flattens a penny, we wondered, what about a rock? When that got boring, we threw them. There were a *lot* of rocks. We found ourselves casing garages and carports, stealing sprinklers, transistor radios, old alarm clocks, and bringing them to the tracks. We stole plywood, four-by-four posts, cinder blocks, and bricks. One day an entire Southern Pacific line backed up and stopped. The conductor hopped off, stick in hand. He wasn't a happy man.

So we moved on. We had a crab apple tree in our front yard, and we stood at the bottom of our driveway, throwing crab apples at cars. We didn't care, Lee and I. Not one bit. When a car's brakes locked and a man jumped out, we didn't even run.

Where the hell do you kids live? he asked.

Here, Lee said.

Y'all are pretty dumb to be throwing rocks at cars in front of your own house.

Fuck you, Lee told this man. They're crab apples.

We'd bike around the neighborhood, just taking stuff. I couldn't stop stealing. If I could slide it down my pants or shirt, I would. I wore sweatpants tucked into my socks, and a large winter coat, even on warm days. On Easter the Good Samaritans hid candy in the woods, and we'd watch from behind trees, wait until they were at church, then take their candy. It was funny, satisfying, full of splendor, and altogether not a bad childhood except every so often my father would appear, wormlike, as if from rotted wood. At first he excited me, for I believed we'd know each other now, but each time he appeared he quickly disappeared again, and I'd find myself on the couch or front porch, watching the street, feeling lonely, empty, incomplete, and wondering what about me drove him away.

Not that he came to Atlanta, no—that's not what piece-of-shit fathers do. Piece-of-shit fathers always make you come to them. I saw him once in Florida when I was four and in New Mexico when I was five, both times with my grampa, and what were these trips like, you might ask? Well, in Florida I remember the water—my grampa liked to swim—and a seafood restaurant. I did not like fish and ordered spaghetti. This bothered my dad. He glanced pointedly at my grampa. Who the fuck, he asked, doesn't like fish? In New Mexico, I noticed a lack of trees, the distance between places, the amount of alcohol they both consumed. In that state, in those days, drunk driving was a full-time job for some people. And my dad did not care. He'd guzzle beer on our way home from the drive-thru liquor store. He lived in a one-room kitchenette on the edge of a vacant stretch of dirt. There were no trees, no shade. In his fridge was only a can of instant coffee, a bag of ginger-snaps, and a six-pack of beer. I feel hesitant describing these men as they drove about the desert, swapping dick jokes and quarreling about the boy in the backseat: What did I realize then? What have I put together over time? They were both tall, hard driven, wore mustaches, and prone to asking people which of them was better looking. Strangers, waitresses, me. Constantly competing, they disagreed about everything—where we went, the places we ate, the money my grampa spent. These arguments involved language I never heard from my mom and Abba—the word "fuck" got tossed around, they ribbed each other often. Any affection or attention from my grampa got labeled "spoiling," "coddling," or "wasteful"; my dad was audibly certain I was "some kind of sissy."

And then something went wrong, I'm not sure what. While grocery shopping, my pop snapped, just lost it. He dragged me out of the store and into the parking lot and began screaming at me. This wasn't a talking-to, sit-down, or time-out, but full-bore rant. Maybe he was drunk, I don't know. He went on and on. I was a dick, an asshole, a fucking-A clown, actually, a jerk, if he shouldn't be swearing, a no-good, never will be, uncouth, if you want the highfalutin. Much louder, and more profound, than anything I'd heard in Atlanta, my father pushed me down by my shoulders and held me, his eyes black as my own, unremitting until my grampa emerged with his liquor and cookies and milk, and then my dad fell silent and remained brooding and unavailable for the rest of my visit.

I WORRIED. What had I done? Was I that unlovable? And worse, what about my dad? Why was he so unhappy? Back in Atlanta, when I didn't hear from him, my worries grew. I called, but he didn't pick up. So I called again, but he didn't answer. He had no answering machine. I called again, but the phone just rang. I called a lot, actually. More than daily. Over and over. Obsessively. As if the act of calling were my goal. Sometimes I'd let the phone ring for six or seven minutes. It would ring, I came to learn that year, longer than I could wait.

My grampa called, at least. Doing great, he reported, still tall, good looking, still swimming every day. Spoke to a young lady at the supermarket yesterday, he'd say. Or at the retirement community. I'm seventy-eight, he'd remind me, but I'll be seventy-nine in six months and three days. Tell that to your pop, he'd say. The old man still has it. And what about my dad? I'd ask. How's he? And my dad was always good, doing great, actually, and then, at that point, always at that point, my grampa would ask to speak to my mom.

I turned six and then seven with no word from my pop. One day I called and the automated recording of a woman answered. She said the number I'd dialed had been disconnected and changed. There was a new number, and I called it, too, but no one answered, and eventually, the automated woman returned and said the number I'd called had been disconnected and was no longer in service. I waited for a new number, but there was none. I called that old number long after it stopped working.

Abba started his own business. It took him on the road. A lot. We familiarized ourselves with Hartsfield Airport, knew its terminals and trains, moving sidewalks and escalators. On our way to the gate, Lee and I raced. Running, I'd yap at my mom, challenging her to show us her speed, and sometimes she would. We owned a small black-and-white TV but could only watch the Braves. Dale Murphy was Lee's favorite. I liked Bob Horner. My mom liked Claudel Washington because of his name. Abba, who was from here, liked Phil Neikro, but old Phil got let go. We were weird. None of us had the same last name. Mine wasn't Macher yet, but something else, something I never saw—I couldn't spell it. This amused my classmates. They laughed. Who can't spell their own last name? I got in a lot of fights. Lee also liked to fight. We'd lock ourselves in a room and beat on each other for hours. In our house, we ate quinoa, tofu, couscous; all of it tasted like ass. Carob chips were popular in our pantry, as were dried apples. We had no soda, no Coca-Cola. We ate rice cakes with unsweetened almond butter and honey. Like I said: we were weird. We didn't go to Disney World or Myrtle Beach but the mountains, where, while Abba and Mom meditated, Lee and I roamed the hillside beating the hell out of each other. In the summer, Aidan visited from Boston, and we went places we didn't normally go—Dairy Queen, the lake, amusement parks—and pitched a tent in our backyard, and all us brothers slept together. Aidan was funny, worldly, older. When he went back to Boston, Lee went, too, then Abba would go on the road for work, leaving my mom in her sadness. Eyes wet, the gate empty late on a Sunday, she didn't want to run now, didn't want to talk. As for me, I continued to steal—sugar products, mostly: sodas, candy, granulated sugar from neighbors' kitchens, slices of fruitcake, but also everyday items such as toy soldiers, back issues of *National Geographic, TV Guide,* and mail—and I waited in the yard every day, hoping a letter might come from my dad that would dazzle me with his great handwriting and wit. Another fall passed, another birthday, another winter, another spring. Clover covered our yard, and I'd count their leaves or find patterns in the clouds, recognizable shapes in the shifting boundaries. On the curb, up in a magnolia tree, or back in the clover, I'd hop on my bike, race down the block looking at mailboxes—flag up and the mailman was late, flag down and he'd already come.

Lee's dad visited, took him to exotic McDonald's and Six Flags. Sometimes I tagged along, but mostly no. Lee grew proficient in ordering off a Chinese menu, spoke often now of yogurt, asked Mom to buy yogurt, only she bought plain yogurt, tart, sugar-free, and so he experimented with many fruit-and-yogurt combos. He liked Erector sets and LEGOs, not soldiers; he built model airplanes. All I cared about was swinging a baseball bat, throwing a baseball, catching one, or horses, stables, barn smells.

And then came the year Lee returned from his dad's making damn sure I knew what "bastard" meant. Now he tossed me on my ass and stomped me. He'd punch me in the belly as I rounded second base or clothesline me on a football field. We fought in front of Mom and Abba and behind closed doors. We fought in our neighbors' houses and at the public swimming pool. I'd like to claim my fair share of licks, but mostly, I just took these beatings as they came to me—one after another. I didn't hate it, not really; I knew what hurt.

Another summer brought another visit from Aidan. Aidan did not beat me. This was both welcome and strange. Did he not love me? Did he not care? Often, I provoked him, but he never budged. No way, he'd say. Why?

He came for two weeks. Each year. Two. That's it. And yet those weeks were glorious—I've described the strange foods we ate—the Taco Bell and the ice creams; we caught fireflies now; watched sunlight dance in the north Georgia pines.

Years passed. I discovered their limits, found out they changed you—my hair browned, I lost teeth. I dreaded my birthday. Did your dad call? people asked.

I showed an innate ability to remember stuff, displayed aptitude in simple math: I was two inches shorter than Lee and two years younger; I'd be taller than him soon. It'd been three years since I heard from my dad.

*　　*　　*

THAT JANUARY, my mom went to the hospital for a few days. While she was gone, her friends came by, watched after Lee and me. Snowfall kept us home from school, and then word came on the radio—there'd been a tragedy with the space shuttle.

After they came back from the hospital, Abba sat me down. You know I don't like to get involved, he said, but it's been a long time since we've heard from your dad. His voice was quiet; he swallowed. We just don't know if he's coming back. Abba had returned from a business trip to be with my mom, and he still wore the suit he'd flown in, though his tie had been pulled free and hung from his breast pocket. I mean, he said. For all we know. But he couldn't say it. He scratched his beard and looked at the ceiling. Well. We just don't know. The last thing I want is to overstep. It's just. I want you to know: if you want a dad, I'll be your dad. I can adopt you, if you let me.

I worried. What about Lee? I asked.

I'd adopt him, too, he said, but he has a father.

OF COURSE, after they changed my last name, my dad was in touch.

Oh, hey, been thinking of you, he said. How're things? What's new?

I told him I liked horses, baseball.

I own a horse, he said, I live on a horse ranch, matter of fact, I went to high school *and college* with a man who owns a Major League Baseball team. Hell of a good guy, actually, you'd love him. How tall are you? he asked.

25

Four foot eight, I said, which was a pretty high number in my grade.

That's cool, he said. I'm six-two.

I called my grampa, as we were still in cahoots then. Guess what, I told him.

Tell me, he said.

Finally heard from that piece of—

Well, well, he said. How wonderful. Shall I call my travel agent?

I'm throwing some stuff in a bag now, I told him, motoring around the house making airplane noises.

Lee got involved. He was building a puzzle. He stood up. What the hell are you doing? he asked.

I'm an airplane, I said.

No, you're not. He slugged me in the belly. You're a whore's son.

TURNS OUT not only did my dad live on a horse ranch, but he trained horses. For money. He slept in a room in the tack house. Pretty cool stuff. Mountains surrounded the ranch. It had this burned-out desert feel; crazy hues colored the sky. In the mornings, my pop worked horses on a lunge-line. I don't remember much of my grampa from this visit. If they argued still, if they'd come to an accord. A moodiness dogged their interactions, I felt certain from my new last name. I knew I was the last male in their line.

After the horses had been worn through, I'd help my dad clean their hooves and wash their backs. Then we'd saddle some animals and ride into the mountains and talk. He was instructional, both loose and stiff, a cigarette always hung from his mouth. Here's how you break an animal, he explained. He spoke of firmness, respect. He spoke of insistence, what's what, how you use your shoulder, you don't back down. He was macho, unfiltered, direct. He inventoried the stable, ordering me to avoid a paint named Stardust. Someone got dirty with her, he said. She ought to be put down. Do not ride. The bitch will throw you.

Thanks, I told him, but I'm a pretty good rider.

The next morning, while my father worked, I brought Stardust into the hills. No sweat. We climbed higher and higher. In the wide gradual trails, I looked down at the ranch and smiled. This was easy. We came to a plateau of pinyon and juniper beyond which the trail steepened and narrowed. Here the horse quit moving.

I nudged her flank. Go on.

But no.

Again I urged her.

She bucked, backed up, hoofed rocks and dust.

The trail's edge dropped a few hundred feet, and she cantered toward it and then stopped abruptly, backed up, raced for it again.

That Brooklyn thing had turned my love of horses inward, and yet I hadn't been lying: I could ride a horse. Calm, cool, collected, I swung my leg over her ass to dismount, but she took off again, full gallop down the trail and into the pinyon stand, where, among the low-hanging branches, she ducked her neck until a branch snatched me out of the saddle and she was gone.

In the dirt, I felt the bottom drop out of my belly.

It was a long walk back on foot. For most of it, I could see the open doors of the equestrian center, a line of horses trotting by. At some point I recognized my dad smoking. Then he spotted me. By the time I got there, he'd mounted his horse.

What did I tell you, he said.

I didn't answer. For a long while we matched eyes.

Finally, he shook his head and glanced over his shoulder. Get on.

But I'd recently learned of a concept called refusal, and was practicing it often. I didn't move.

Son, he said. If you don't get on this horse, it's over between us.

His boots filled the stirrups. How'm I to get on? I asked.

He kicked loose a foot, hands tight on the reins, posture erect.

I got on, held his shoulders as we bounced up the trail.

Of course my pop knew exactly where Stardust was—grazing junipers in that same pinyon stand. There're wild horses up here, he scoffed. I think she's in heat. Go on now, he said. Get off. Go get her.

I refused to dismount. That horse tried to kill me.

I don't care, he said. March your ass over there and get back on her.

You can't make me.

His lip curled. Son, he said, this is not very becoming, I must say. You shouldn't have ridden her in the first place. And blah-blah your mother, he said, or something like that. And blah-blah your grampa! He lowered his face close to my own. That damn horse won't buck around me. You can bet on that!

Two things. One: I rode Stardust back down the mountain, but I would never get on a horse again. Sliding off her, back at the stable, I called out to my dad. By now, he was brushing his horse down, a cigarette hanging from his mouth. He did not look up at me. Hey, I said again. Dad. I get it. It's a lesson.

Oh yeah? he asked, still not looking up. What did you learn?

That you're an asshole.

The second thing isn't even part of this story, but I'll mention it anyway: the next summer, while Lee was in Boston with his dad and Abba was out of town, my mom and me drove to Florida. She said we were going to Disney World. I'd never been. And I thought, you know, cool, finally we're doing something normal. But near Orlando, she changed her mind. Instead of going to Disney World, she drove me to my grampa's house. I was ten years old. We stayed one night. I did not see my grampa again until my twenties.

AFTER THE HORSE VISIT, I didn't hear from my dad. For a while. I'd call and get the usual nothing or that automated woman. These were the years when Bobby Cox took over the Braves' front office. He traded first Bob Horner and then Dale Murphy. He shipped Doyle Alexander to the Tigers for a double-A righty named John Smoltz. Gant, Glavine, Blauser, and Lemke materialized from Richmond. Farm reports mentioned a sweet-swinging lefty as well, David Justice. In 1990 Cox would draft the great Chipper Jones, fire Russ Nixon, appoint himself field manager, and begin a run of success like no other, but all that came later.

The differences between me and Lee broadened. He wasn't so down for baseball, did terribly in school. He grew his hair out and wore a hat pulled low over his eyes. Meanwhile, I seemed to thrive. Tall, with quick hands, I had a natural inclination toward violence—sports were revelatory. And yet I was unhappy, I rarely fit in; I switched schools, switched again. Always the new kid, I fought one boy after another until someone befriended me. I got good grades, scored in the highest percentile on all your standardized tests. There was talk of sending me to a magnet school. Duke and Princeton sent letters, had me take more tests, tests I aced. I had a bright future. Teachers wrote gushing notes to my mother speaking of my "promise" and calling me "gifted," "special," and, worst of all: "full of potential."

Despite this, I felt *less than* always, vague even, hazy. I lacked something inside, and no accolade could replace it. Between tests and games, I'd sit in a brooding stupor, completely empty, or go about the house lording my potential over Lee. His beatings took on a different tone. Rarely severe, always unpredictable, they confounded the idea I had of myself—not everything came easy.

But then Lee bowled me over in the neighbor's yard one day, left me gasping to breathe. Next to me was a baseball bat. I grabbed it, came up swinging. His eyes bulged. He sprinted for the house, but I chased him, swinging the bat across the street and up our driveway and through the garage and kitchen and den, caught him at his bedroom. He ducked just before I smashed apart the door's threshold. I bashed holes in the wall all around that door.

AT SOME POINT my pops got in touch, and I visited him for the first time alone. He lived in a Tuscan hacienda outside Santa Fe. It felt like a compound, easily the nicest home I'd ever seen, had all the bells and whistles—high adobe walls, iron gates, with a multi-story open kitchen, an enormous slate mantel, marble and wide-plank hardwood flooring, a sauna in the guest wing, a Jacuzzi in the master bath, picture windows, expansive views, a bubbling brook stocked with steelhead, an outdoor wet bar, a pond built, it seemed, for nothing.

Whoever owned this place had plenty of disposable income.

This is not my home, he said right off, but my roommate's. He's away, he added. I just live here.

During long drives in the desert, he told me things. His dog was named after a literary hero, he still owned the horse, his car ran on diesel. He liked beer backed by tequila and smoked unfiltered cigarettes, four packs a day. He smoked while he drove and drank while he drove and smoked in bed long after he thought I'd fallen asleep. He liked to read, didn't follow sports or TV, listened to classical music, spoke Spanish fluently. With sun-browned skin, he looked almost exotic, as if he were from somewhere else, but he was born in L.A. and raised in Richmond. We were Black Irish, he said, almost completely. His grandma, my great-grandma, came over at the turn of the century, settled in Indiana, where she ran an Irish boarding-house. She was a gambler, her husband a gambler, she made extra money hosting card games in her cellar, had four sons who all went to Purdue; her husband, my great-grampa, died in a card game, got shot in the head, was dumped in the river. My grampa was a genius, a mad scientist, almost opaque—the lead engineer, my dad said, on Reynolds Wrap.

My dad had attended an elite boarding school, an Ivy League college, and numerous deb balls, had the gorgeous handwriting—he was polished, in other words, and good looking, educated, well spoken, international, even: he'd lived in New York, San Francisco, Toronto, Los Angeles, and Buenos Aires—which meant I'd need to achieve these things, as well. You might not get an invitation to anyone's coming out party, my dad suggested, but you can damn well work on that penmanship of yours. His mom was straight off the boat, and hadn't been in his life much when he was a child, he hadn't known her as an adult, only saw her a couple of times, and not in, God, fifteen years. He didn't know where she was now, he claimed. Possibly back in Ireland. Or in an institution again. Probably dead.

But I met her once, I said.

No, you didn't. His tone was bitter, angry. Then doubt crept in: *Where?*

In a cab. In New York City. That time.

That wasn't my mother, he said.

Who was it, then?

It doesn't matter, he snarled. She's dead.

We were headed north for green mountains shrouded by a coming storm. Lightning fractured the sky. Our windows were cracked just enough for smoke to slip through, it was a beautiful, bleary, pre-rain desert day, and yet this tonal change of his—how he'd go from zero to angry so quickly—brought to mind all my worries.

Dad, I said. Why are you so unhappy?

I'm not, he said. Who told you this? Your mother?

Is it because you smoke? I asked.

He pulled off the road, fists tight on the steering wheel. He closed his eyes as if with a headache, then opened them and stared at the inky horizon. I tell you what, he said. Three things in this world bring me joy. Beer. My dog. Cigarettes. He turned to me, a smile forming. Oh, he said. One other thing. I like horses. That's it.

He also liked to drive. Each day we drove somewhere new. We went to pueblos on plateaus and museums, walked dusty arroyos, sat in cathedrals. On one drive a man joined us. He was nice, soft-spoken, well dressed and groomed. I liked him. My dad clearly liked him, too. They balanced each other, one happy and one brooding. Coming back, we stopped at a package store, and that night, as they drank by the pond, I watched them laugh and listened to them speak in a fast Spanish I couldn't understand. Their interaction enthralled me, my father enthralled me—the way his hands moved, the subtle flick of his fingers as he ashed a cigarette. Everything he did fascinated me, how ash collected at the end of a cherry, and sometimes—when he told a story—he'd forget to ash, and I'd stop hearing his words, this ash my only concern. What would happen to it? How long could it get before falling? And what if it fell on him? Would it hurt?

I didn't hear the transition to English, just felt that dubious gaze of his. Come on, he said, shaking his head at me. We need to do this.

Oh, his friend told him. Let it go.

No. It's time he learned.

My dad took me into the kitchen, got a fork, knife, and empty plate. You have to learn, he said. He grabbed my fingers and bent them around the handle of the fork, took my other hand, formed those fingers around the handle of the knife.

I wasn't sure of his point and asked him, but he just swore.

In the post-dusk desert quiet, his voice boomed. Why can't you fucking-A learn?

Every time he exploded caught me unaware—like we were just bouncing along, a father and his adoring son, and now he said this: What is wrong with you?

There was no steak in front of me, no potato on a plate. It was all imaginary.

How do you eat at home? Is this what you do? What's your mom been doing all these years?

This stuff, I said, tossing the utensils on the floor, is stupid to me.

A YEAR PASSED WITH NO WORD. Now I was eleven, a pretty big deal, actually—five foot ten, handsome smile, a full head of hair. Six weeks after my birthday, I came home to find an envelope with gorgeous handwriting on the kitchen table.

Well, looky here, I told Lee. Look whose piece-of-shit father remembered his birthday this year, and I began prancing in front of him, doing the piece-of-shit-father dance. What about your piece-of-shit father, did your piece-of-shit father remember your birthday?

My mom came into the room. Even Abba.

Go on, Lee said, smiling. Let's see what your piece-of-shit father has to say.

Should I read it aloud? I asked him.

Please do, Lee said.

No, my mom said. Sweetie. No.

Lee, Abba said, come outside with me.

Yeah, I told Lee. Goodbye!

The letter began fairly basic: Dear Son, Hope you're well and liking school. Grampa tells me you're playing baseball. That's great. I don't know much about baseball but I'm glad you've found something you love doing. For a few sentences, he hemmed and hawed over a variety of perceived slights—blah-blah, in other words, your mom, and so forth; it was an old story, one he often degenerated to in those years, as if her shortcomings spurred his own and without which he would've been involved in my life—before cutting to the chase: Son, this is a difficult letter to write. As you may know, I don't have girlfriends and never married. You might also notice I have a lot of male friends. You're obviously somewhat smart sometimes in certain areas and may've guessed already—I am gay. I don't want you to worry. I'm not sick, not dying. I'm in perfectly good health. The only reason I'm telling you this now is your brothers' father has decided to tell Lee and Aidan about my sexuality, as he is a homophobe, probably latent and/or closeted, what's known as a charlatan or pretender—we can talk about this later—and I don't want you hearing it from your brothers, as I know how kids can be. So, there it is. I'm sure you have many questions, though if you don't that's okay, too. I'm available to talk should you need to. I want you to know I'm proud of who I am, and I want you to be proud of me, too. Love, Pop.

I felt relieved. He was gay, so what. He was okay. I thought his coming out would change things, that he'd no longer keep me at arm's length, for I believed the two were related—his strange disappearances were simple protection, a product of his fierce privacy—and now, things being clear, we'd carry on as normal father and son.

I folded the letter into its envelope and pocketed it. My mom watched me. Abba, too. Even Lee had come back into the room, an apple in his hand.

So, Lee said, biting the apple. Tell us. What did the letter say?

You know what it said, I told him.

He finished chewing and smiled. I really don't. Tell me. Please, I'd love to know.

It says your father is a real piece of shit. Nothing new there.

At least he's not a fag, Lee said, and then he did something very Lee-like, which I've come to think of more than anything else that happened that night. He punched me in the stomach, ran out the door, and disappeared into the woods across the street.

SO BEGAN MY BEST YEARS. I made friends. Real friends. Every day we'd go into the woods and shoot things, set fires, and blow stuff up. There were a lot of fights and fishing, a lot of breaking and entering. We vandalized cars, houses, buildings, played basketball, football, baseball, home-run derby, twenty-one, horse, smear the queer, anything. They all had older brothers with cars and spare time. Most nights I only came home for dinner, if at all. I spent weeks straight at my friends' homes, knew their parents better than my own. Hair grew on my balls, above my lip. I was six-one, six-two, a beast in local Pop Warner leagues. At fourteen, I could dunk two-handed from a standstill and throw a baseball very, very hard. Something else came about. One night me and the guys found ourselves at Shayla's house. Shayla was well developed for that age. And her mom was some rocker chick, a real backstage Betty, who wore Daisy Duke bottoms with bikini tops and peroxide hair; a sweet lady, really. She'd decorated their house with half-naked photos of herself posed on a motorcycle or the hood of some car—she still features prominently in my occasional wet dream. Roach clips dangled from bent hooks on the wall. A python slithered freely from room to room. Her fridge was stocked with beer, a handle of vodka chilled in her freezer. I brazenly sauntered through the kitchen, opened the freezer, and removed a bottle. What a feeling to pour a few fingers and drink. This was something else entirely. For the first time in my life, I knew exactly who I was: this. I finished my glass and filled it again. Where had this been all these years?

From then on, I drank as much as often as quickly as possible, each time trying to set a record—I'd get there faster than anyone had before. Drunk, I didn't worry. Didn't care. I was funny and much better-looking drunk. I knew what to say, how fast to say it. I became that fool who brings a handle of vodka to beer pong. As much as I liked being drunk, being blacked out was much, much better. Then I didn't think anymore.

Well. Colleges stopped sending me letters. Magnet schools no longer asked me to shadow their students. Quickly, and in earnest, once high school started, I got kicked out of all my honors classes and all my AP-what-have-you. I didn't care. Drinking was what I'd do now. It was something I was good at, and loved. I'd still go to Harvard, of course, or Yale, but high school—shit.

Lee, too, had gone now, left for Boston to live with his piece-of-shit father. We'd stopped speaking by then, though I heard various reports of him drifting beyond the peripherals—he'd left his father's house, dropped out of school, stayed with strangers or friends. Then he was homeless in a city park. And then no one knew.

THAT SUMMER MY FRIENDS AND I adopted a new point of emphasis, which was the shopping mall. Someone had clued us in—girls hung out there. We roamed around, drenched in Polo, Obsession, Drakkar Noir. I recall violently tongue-kissing a girl in front of a mattress display. As when drunk, a feeling of self-worth emerged. It was like Kevlar, or a coordinated growth spurt. It plugged the emptiness I felt inside. Ten feet tall and bulletproof, adaptable to any social setting, I had no clue how to take it easy. School suspended me now and then. I caught a semester of detention, failed every class, was academically ineligible for basketball, baseball—next thing I knew, we had a for-sale sign in our yard.

Is it true, the guys asked, are you moving?

Yeah, I said, I guess.

Where to?

California.

My friends' parents pulled me into their kitchens and garages. I hear you're leaving, they said. Is this what you want? If you don't want to go, you can stay here with us. We can work something out.

But my dad had moved to California by then, to Palm Springs. And I told people my dad lived there, which is the kind of thing people understand. Then I called him and he answered.

Guess what, I said. I'm six-four now.

Uh-huh.

You know what that means?

He offered only the crackle of a burning cigarette.

I'm two inches taller than you. Want to know something else?

What? he said.

We're moving again. To the Bay Area. That's right, Pop. We're going to be close. I'll get to see you all the time. I'm a visit regular, maybe spend summers with you, possibly move in permanently. Tell me about Palm Springs. Good schools there? I'm coming this week, going to check the place out. Should I dogleg south and we rendezvous?

SURE ENOUGH, the day I turned fifteen, a month after moving to California, I came home from baseball practice and found an envelope with gorgeous handwriting. It was, no lie, one of two times he'd remembered my birthday. This was new, the real thing, a change—no more fear of vulnerability, no continent of separation to guard against. My legs shook, my stomach lurched, I was excited—I'd be close to my dad now, our closeness would complete me.

Our mailbox was at the bottom of a steep hill, and I read the letter walking up it, though once the words began forming coherent sentences, I stopped and looked about. My mom's car was gone. Abba was out of town. Was this real? I read the letter from beginning to end and then again. I turned it in my hands—was there more? A smiley face, perhaps, a "just joking," an "April Fool's," something, fucking anything, other than this—

I read it again. And again. But all it said was what his actions had been telling me all these years: he didn't love me, he was tired of pretending, he didn't want to hear from me again, and had asked his family not to contact me; in short, so long, goodbye, and fuck off.

I walked back down the hill to our trash cans and threw the thing away.

I'd never speak to him again.

Then and Now

POUR my mom a few chardonnays and she might tell you some stories. That year was unkind to both of us. I drank a lot. More than too much. Blackout-style always, no kidding. Once I drove her car halfway off a bridge. For a while she watched me fall apart. Then we stopped speaking, and I only saw her in passing, like around town, early in the morning, me scuffed and dampened, jeans torn, out all night drinking. But she was not sad anymore. She was tough. After a bender got me kicked off the basketball team, she sent me to boarding school. This way you won't kill anyone driving, she said. Don't you think?

It's funny—not the dreams I had, but my ways of reaching them. I planned to play college baseball. Didn't have to be the Ivy Leagues anymore, just somewhere. But before I left, I stole a bunch of weed from some guy. Enough to make me popular, if I hadn't smoked it all myself. Still, here I was—at boarding school, just like my pop. Not Andover, of course, but nearby. And at boarding school, I was good enough to start varsity as a sophomore. I batted third in the lineup, played center field, was a run producer and line-drive hitter, made all-league, honorable mention. And what else? I liked a girl, but she did not know my name. That's fine, I thought, as I left campus that May. Next year, I'll be a junior. Next year, I'll make first team all-league, the colleges will start calling, and I'll get to keep playing a few more seasons. Next year, I'll bring even more weed.

THE FIRST I ENCOUNTERED any of this recovery business was that summer, when I worked for a moving and storage facility. The rest of the guys who worked there all had nine months clean, or once did, but were now fresh off benders that had seen their women gather their children and go. They lived in boardinghouses in condemned buildings in decaying neighborhoods or in snail-backs on a pasture's edge far from town. They wore court-issued ankle bracelets. Their vehicles wouldn't start if they couldn't blow clean into a tube. They caught rides or hitchhiked or filled their radiators halfway to the docks. I thought they were cool, their coolness proof of my own; we shared a common vision for how life ought to be—existing on the peripherals, the margins, we were outliers who'd solved the riddle and so forth—there is no set way, no limit, life is full of options and freedom.

A hard-dick named Rick D. ran the place, and he pulled me aside, issued a warning like Stay the fuck away from those guys, but I didn't listen. After work, I followed them into the parking lot, where they sullenly smoked me out before pushing me away. Aren't you listening? they'd explain. Haven't you heard a word we've said? You don't want this.

But I did.

I returned to campus carrying a few pounds, at least. Now

that girl I liked knew exactly who I was, and when she saw me, she'd say things, little things, I admit, but things—Where are you going? What are you doing this weekend?

I *think* she liked me.

One night we went for a walk and, afterward, made plans to meet behind Cumbies that Friday night, but the dean of students moved me out of the dorms and into his house, and I hot-boxed his bathroom and vandalized his property, and Friday morning they sent me home. They weren't kicking me out, they said, just giving me a breather, some time to think. We'll let you know, they told my mom. In a few weeks. Kid's got a chemical-dependency issue.

For a while, I donked around my mom's town, waiting for a decision. I knew whatever they decided would lead my mom to her own decisions, and I didn't want to know what that looked like. You might think this meant I took it easy, but I'd become the worst kind of kid—fearless and empty—and there isn't anything you can do about a boy like that but get out of the way.

And what actions did I take to prove my contrition? And how did I go about getting in shape for baseball season? Well, I recall quite a few hazy evenings, fifth of off-brand vodka in one hand, packed bowl in the other, going into and coming out of one blackout or another in such varied locales as the water, the highway, and several notorious homeless encampments. I'd come to on a park bench or couch, sort of explaining the physics of hitting, the two planes that are a thrown baseball and swung bat, a sixty-forty weight split from front to back leg, and the mechanics of chopping a tree, the fishing hook, or an inside-out swing.

Or I drove the winding, hallucinatory Pacific Coast Highway, looking for mushrooms or some hitchhiker, always too fucked up to notice anyone else on the road, and instead just focused on the yellow grass, the empty blue sky above dusty eucalyptus on whatever distant ridge. I'd pull over to roll a joint or throw up and hold myself to the reedy brush, puking until I cramped. One day I found myself wandering an apricot orchard in the San Joaquin. I closed my eyes. When I opened them, I was sitting on a couch in front of a TV next to an old man, a stranger. His pants were halfway down his thighs. He had a fully erect dick in his hand—his own—and was pointing it at me.

God damn it, I told him.

Just hold steady, my friend, he said, nodding like a foot-in-the-door salesman with only positive affirmations. Nice. You got it. You're a natural. Don't move.

A porn played on the TV. A regular old fuck-film—just two people banging, nothing unusual. On a cutting board on the coffee table was a handle of rum, a pound of brick weed, and a butcher's knife. I stood up.

Where you going? he said. This ain't weird.

That's cool, I said. But it's not for me.

I backed out of his apartment, not knowing where I was or where I'd left my car, though as I began walking, things grew clear. I'd come to the Mission to see the house I'd been born in. I must have gone on some drunken sentimental quest.

I stole a few shorties of rum from a corner store and jittered up one road and down the next, looking over my shoulder and ahead until I found my car, got behind the wheel, downed the short dogs, browned out, came to in heavy traffic, stepped on the gas, and no!

Red light. Rear-ended a Cadillac.

Four dudes jumped out wearing black leather jackets, with slicked and crisp dark hair, Mediterranean features.

I got out, too, but they surrounded me before I could run.

Who the fuck are you? they asked.

I don't know. Nobody, I guess.

Is that your bumper?

It was my bumper. I picked it up and tossed it at the curb. One of them made a joke and the others laughed. They got back in their Caddy and sped away.

THAT NIGHT the school called my mom. Apparently, they'd found out about some bikes I'd stolen. He's done here, they said. Good luck.

Fuck them, I said when she told me.

Oh, really? One of her eyebrows arched. Were it me, I'd prosecute.

Well, it ain't you, I said.

But she's a funny woman. Even now, whenever she hears me claim I dropped out of high school, she's the first to correct me. Kicked out, she says. Got kicked out of preschool, too. Like I said, she's tough.

Listen to me, she said. Listen very carefully. If you drink again in my house, you're gone.

I decided to go down to the docks, see about my old summer job. Old Rick D. didn't even look up from his paperwork. I thought you were a junior, he scoffed.

Was, I said proudly.

Give you a piece of advice, he said. I knew you'd be back.

He had a real intuition about things, mostly from dealing with the men who worked for him. Many mornings, we had no idea who'd actually show up. Rick D. monitored the scanners before assigning work detail or sent me to the water to look for bodies. The guys who did show smelled of beer, vomit, and BO. Around the coffeepot, they spoke in dated resentments—old what's-her-face, alimony, child support, the beast that is dope, the motherfucker who is methamphetamine.

Of course I thought all this made me tough and shit real. This was a new chapter, maybe a bleak one, but only a chapter, and soon things would turn again, but the truth is, I wasn't tough and shit was not real. Not yet. Later, maybe. In 1994 I was simply a loser.

Across the street from the warehouse, a liquor store sold dirt weed at sixty dollars an ounce, less than half of what I got for it in school. A few weeks' work, I figured, and I'd buy a bushel of this schwag, bring it back east. Maybe, if I sold enough, I could link up with that girl, get her to drop some cotton on me. I was a virgin.

So I bought a lot of weed. Then bragged on my plans to these old heroes. That's fine, they said. Now just pass me that fucking joint.

But, I said, listen.

No, they said. I like you better when you don't talk.

But about this plan of mine—

No, they said. Your voice. It ruins my high.

WELL, I RARELY REMEMBER my dreams these days, but every so often I have one where I'm playing high school baseball

46

again. There's always a blue sky, green grass, a fifteen-foot chain-link fence. It's not the home run that clouds my dreams but the aftermath, out there in the field, punching my mitt, still feeling that fleeting freedom of rounding the bases at an easy pace.

One day I got off work, hotter than balls, I remember, Indian summer, warehouseman polyesters clinging to my body, slight breeze on my nape, a pay phone, an empty sky, that girl's voice. I told her exactly what would happen, how I'd get my shit in order and come east and they'd let me back in school, two, three weeks, tops, but later that day or maybe the next morning, I came out of a blackout doing 110 on a downhill, and then again on the PCH somewhere with my car pressed into a hillside, and once more at the airport, where Lee and his girlfriend were sitting on their luggage, cigarettes in their mouths and arms crossed, waiting for me. It'd been a while for him and me; his hair hung past his shoulders, piercings covered his girlfriend's face. He didn't even say hello, just circled the car, skeptical of its dented sidewalls and missing fender. Mom seen this? he asked, and I told him no, and his girlfriend laughed and asked was I okay, like to drive, but I was fine, I explained, just fine. Don't worry, I said. I do this all the time. And I was fine, decent, anyway, maybe not sober yet, but only vaguely drunk, the blackouts gone, and good to drive. I steered with my knee while rolling a joint, lit and huffed it and offered them some, but they waved me off. Lee averted his eyes.

Before you even say it, I told him, I have a plan. And then I told him my plan, same plan I'd told the girl. I just need a few weeks, two or three, tops.

Lee turned in his seat and raised an eyebrow at his girl. A long way to go for a booty call, he said.

They laughed. Then they started screaming. And I turned back to the road.

I was in the wrong lane. Going the wrong way. Headed straight on for a Chevy Suburban. So I stepped on the brakes.

Nothing happened.

We kept moving. And moving.

I couldn't stop the car. No matter what I tried. It kept hurtling forward.

Jesus, I thought. My mom was right. I was going to die. And Lee, too. And his girlfriend. And whoever was in the Suburban. We were all going to die.

The hood crinkled. The entire front of my car jumped back at the windshield—the carburetor, all the plugs and hoses, the engine all rushed at me—

And then everything stopped.

I peeled my cheek off the windshield, touched my face and chest—no blood. I jumped from the car. The other driver hadn't moved. Her hands frozen around the wheel, mouth agape, she'd been screaming but run out of voice.

We got lucky. My car was half its original size.

THAT NIGHT THE POLICE CAME, watched me pack a bag. I was sleeping in a room above a detached garage, and once I finished packing, the police escorted me down the steps and to the street. My mom came out to the porch but wouldn't look at me. Abba emerged. He crossed the lawn to the police cruiser and handed me an envelope with a one-way plane ticket inside.

You can take the bus to the airport, Abba said. From there you have two options—you can either go to this home we've arranged for you to live in and get help, or be on your own in the world. But you can't live here anymore.

I looked at my mom then, but she shook her head, her eyes wet, firm, angry. You could have killed four people today, she said, before turning to go in.

In Salt Lake, on a three-hour layover, my head cleared. I didn't care. That's what I realized. I just wanted out of this somehow. I wanted to get away. In the smoking room, watching the runway, I sucked down a pack of cigarettes. I still had a brick of weed or two. Snow fell, snowdrifts piled at the edges of the tarmac, lights bounced in this falling snow. A digital screen displayed departures, many of them headed for Atlanta. I wondered how many were full, if Delta might change my flight. Then I thought about that girl—I wanted to see her again. Funny. I don't even remember her name now.

Boys' Home

THE rest of the boys were the usual ages except the oldest, who was twenty-four and cool. I guess he used to be some child actor but then wasn't a child anymore and would linger in alleys off Santa Monica Boulevard, hustling dick to score. I'll tell you what happens, he said, you stay down this road.

Hold on, I told him. Let me find a pen. I'ma write this shit down.

Go on, he said. If you don't believe me! You'll see. One day they're hand-feeding you lobster while you bang someone in the mouth, and the next you're on your knees, clawing sperm from your beard. What happens is—

Shh, someone said. Enough.

I counted seven other boys. A few of them mentioned being court-ordered, sent by the state. Others, like me, spoke of good situations. From their bunks, they watched me or didn't care at all. Outside, wind whistled down from whatever mountain ranges surrounded us. Air passed around the single-pane glass. It was cold.

You're in a safe place, the child actor said. It works if you work it, God willing, one day at a time.

Above me, our youngest shifted uneasily in his bunk. This boy probably grew up to become a world-class carpet muncher and finger fucker—he had a scientists' curiosity about cause and effect—but he was thirteen and barely pubescent and used his intellectual curiosity in despicable ways. He'd squat outside the mess hall, a perfect leaf of iceberg lettuce in his hands, luring small rabbits, and then—once they got close—he'd jab a pitchfork into their spines. But I didn't know him yet and just figured he was restless.

I asked, How long—

Hey, new guy, someone cut me off. Shut the fuck up.

Guys laughed. This one dude, Visalia, talked about the Central Valley. It's Disneyland, he explained, for your common tweaker. He was jocular, intense; he kept going on and on about the town—Visalia—he called home, boasting it claimed the purest crystal in all of California. After a while I began to understand that he was doing this to work our nerves.

Above me, the young boy sighed faintly with discontent. He hopped off our bunk and slipped into the bathroom.

I felt the wind even when I didn't hear it; my belly ached; I couldn't get warm. I thought about the ride from the airport, that one-lane from the regional airport I'd flown into, the ranches we'd passed, their long driveways and snowy lawns, smoke billowing from their chimneys. Some already had lights up, plastic reindeer on their roofs. What were my odds of finding something here? Not booze, weed, or pills, but NyQuil, maybe.

Wheezing, the young boy crept across the cabin, stopping at one of the bunks. What the shit, Visalia said, his nasal voice whiny and shrill. There was noise. A lot of it. Terrible stuff.

Beds squeaked, rocked, guys jumped from their bunks. Someone got slapped. The lights popped on. Visalia, who was a big boy—much bigger than me—pulled the young boy by his rattail up onto a bunk, where he spanked at his ass and lectured on how things would be. This isn't kid shit, he said. It's not kid time. This'll be every day.

Shaving cream coated Visalia's face, caked his forehead, and cuffed his ears. He wrist-wiped his eyes, wrapped his giant hands around the boy's throat, and began the slow, arduous task of choking him to death.

LATER IN THE DARKNESS, as if nothing had happened, the child actor began again. Something, something, he whispered, Santa Monica. I thought he was talking in his sleep, but no. He listed a bit of his résumé, prominent TV shows, a few commercials—was he bragging, I wondered, should I hate him? He was good-looking, pretty, with a small nose, blue eyes, and pink cheeks. He wore a full beard, had thick blond hair. He owned rugged boots and fancy wool socks, things I coveted, but there wasn't anything to hate. He was just enthusiastic, that's all. He spoke of other places he'd been, all of them fancier than here, what with their girls and grapes and swimming pools, yet in each place he'd found only more of himself, and each place had brought him back to that well-choreographed dance— head bowed, hands cuffed, not so exuberant now. He spoke of cunning and patience, an omnipresent, ever-darkening thing. You can bet on me this time, he said, or I'll be in the grave. What happens, he said, is shit gets worse and then worse again and even worse until finally worse still. But his clothes fit, his

53

beard was manicured, he was represented by a top-tier talent agency, and his parents hadn't given up on him.

I turned in my bed. Outside, snow fell but just slightly, a hazy flurry of speckled flakes, a dusting really, just a dusting, but it didn't stop, and by morning snowdrifts would pile around our cabin. It was Thanksgiving. I reached up and touched the slats above me, felt grooves where boys had carved their names, hometowns, admit dates. The dates were always just the first day with a dash, as if they planned on coming back and inscribing their last day, but last days always changed or guys swapped cabins and forgot.

IT WAS A TEN-THOUSAND-ACRE working ranch in an obscure valley in the Rocky Mountains. Cattle guards pocked a dirt road running through it. Livestock fencing surrounded our living quarters. There were a few barns, a stable, pump- and outhouses, a septic building, a tack room and bunkhouse, prefabs with corrugated steel roofs and corrugated siding where we met with social workers; in a ten-wide, we took diagnostics. The ranch had Clydesdales, rusted farm trucks, a basketball hoop. An old house with its windows blown out and upstairs cordoned off had been converted to a rumpus room with a Ping-Pong table and weight bench, a woodstove its only source of heat. In surrounding fields and woods were straw-and-sod structures so old and run-down I couldn't guess their original use. It was desolate, beautiful—evergreens covered the snowy mountains that rose pristine on the far horizon.

There were no TVs or radios; nothing hung from the walls in our cabins. We couldn't read, listen to music, or follow the

news. We couldn't talk on the phone; there were no comput-
ers. Entertainment came in the form of masturbation, fuckaround-fuckaround, and late-night hijinks.

They called it voluntary, and though windows opened freely,
doors remained unlocked, there were no guard towers or razor
wire, and we could leave, technically, if we wanted, I've come
to think of the word "voluntary" as quite a bit different now.
It was twenty miles to the nearest gas station, even farther to
a bus depot. No taxis passed. No nearby neighbors meant no
nearby cars to steal. Hitchhiking was possible, guys did it, but
winter in that pocket of America can be unkind to people
caught on the road. Glorified orderlies, called night techs,
and social workers came and went in weather-beaten SUVs
I'd stare at longingly, imagining myself behind the wheel with
only the continent in front of me, but the techs carried small
arms—Glocks, Berettas, .25s—and the social workers removed
their car batteries at the start of each shift. All of them knockaround types and former cons who'd seen it all, they'd peer
over a cigarette, tell us how lucky we were—you oughta seen
Father Mike's outside Pittsburgh. Oh, hell no, this ain't no
home. Homes are blah-blah a Quonset hut, one two three
hundred bunks in all, guys gagging you in the shower and—
But they never finished the thought.

I'M NOT SURE WHO TRULY BELIEVED, who was just getting
paid. They tossed us stacks of paperwork, all of it intro-level,
basic, fill-in-the-blanks—list examples of powerlessness, write an
essay on your own insanity. Then they'd jack the heat up, offer
Kleenex. Letters from our parents called this "treatment," said

from it we'd get fixed, and we'd sit about the porch, cigarettes frozen to our lips, with spit-crusted beards and wind-bit eyes, reading these letters aloud. Huh. Is that so?

We shoveled ice, dug slabs of granite from the earth, and moved them. Rock has never been moved so ambivalently from one pile to another, digging it up, taking it out, digging and putting it back, continuously this movement for hours on end, as if the act of excavation were the only goal, and who knows—people say idle hands are the devil's dick skinners—maybe it was. Like the child actor, boys who'd been other places told stories of fruit baskets, fancy cheeses, swimming pools, blow jobs off the eighteenth green, but if that happened here, I didn't see it. We played chess, Ping-Pong, slap and tickle, perpetrated cup checks, flushed empty toilets while boys showered, lifted weights, and smoked many a cigarette staring out at pastures, evergreens, and mountains, a low gray or high blue sky, all of it striking, full or vacant, perfectly lighted or bleak, intriguing and desolate. There'd been a pool once, but it had long since been drained and filled in with rocks other boys had moved and poured over with ready-mix and grouted so all that remained was an iced-over slab other boys would one day break apart. We cut down trees, carried them on our shoulders, four five six boys to a tree, set them on sawhorses, shaved their bark, sanded, primed, and painted them, or walked behind farm trucks pitchforking hay and tossing it over our shoulders.

It felt like a work camp, a boys' home.

THEY WANTED US TO TALK and share our feelings but, no disrespect, that's not for me. In group, I hid behind my hair, or by pretending to pay close attention, or spacing out. They always had agendas. How about your biological father? they'd ask. How do you feel about him?

Fine.

C'mon, Tommy. The group can help.

Naw, I said. Thanks and all, but naw.

This, they claimed, was pure disease. They got threatening: If you don't talk about him, you'll drink again.

How's that follow? It didn't seem logical. And besides. That guy said it himself—he's done with me. You should see the letter he wrote.

Tell us about the letter.

Naw, I'd say, for it was shameful to me, and didn't fit with my delusions of what I meant to him.

They'd elongate a silence, look at us with their piercing eyes, smoke shrouding their faces, a kind of smile both sad and amused.

It was not uncommon for the young boy to gather snowballs and sticks, rocks or frozen cow dung, and hide behind the septic tank, waiting for half-asleep boys to stumble along. He stood five foot three—too young to have hit any growth spurt or too stunted by the gasoline he'd huffed—and weighed no more than eighty-five pounds, a perfect waif, really. Most days, returning to our cabin, I'd find him bandied about as if a Frisbee. He'd careen off a bunk and into the arms of someone who'd choke him to his knees or slap at and sucker-punch him. But he didn't care. That's the thing. He didn't give a shit. He'd reach into the stall and snake your toilet paper while you shat or kick you square in the ass while you peed.

The child actor was bisexual, the young boy a sociopath,

Visalia schizophrenic. I liked Visalia. This couldn't be true. Is it? I asked him.

It is, he said.

A thought occurred. What does that even mean?

It means I'm crazy, he said.

How does that happen? I asked.

And then he told me.

I PREPARED TO RUN, practicing the same simple math I'd practiced for years—buy an ounce for sixty, sell a quarter for thirty-five—and counted the days until I could leave, whipping a shovel like a baseball bat—step, hip, hands—always keeping the spade inside the ball. In a pair of boots in my mom's house was a pound of dirt weed worth a grand if I broke it into eighths and sold it on the East Coast. I'd go back to Georgia, I figured, maybe boarding school, find that pretty girl, and bang her on her knees.

Send me those boots, I wrote my mom. It's cold here. Lots of snow. I can never stay warm.

THEY EXAMINED AND BATTERED US, looking for disorders beyond the normal drug- and alcohol-induced insanity, patterns within those disorders, whatever new normalcy emerged—we studied ink blots, suffered psychiatrists—one test had six hundred true/false questions. They gave us an hour to complete it. Some of it made sense. Like: Once in a while I think of things too bad to talk about. My father was a good man. Or, if he is still living, my father *is* a good man. At times, I have very much wanted to leave home. And yet most of it was weird: I like dirt. I used to like drop-the-handkerchief.

They administered the test in a ten-wide trailer on the edge of a pasture. We used number two pencils. While waiting, boys played war, UNO, chess: I am troubled by attacks of nausea and vomiting. I would like to be a singer. I feel that it is certainly best to keep my mouth shut when I'm in trouble. At times, I feel like swearing.

I see different sides of things, duality, alternate interpretations, think of words as less than rules, the boundaries of their definitions fluid, such as "seldom" and "troubled."

I'd be lying straight up if I denied the poetry in some questions, their intuition, enigma, and power. At their clearest, they were true, undeniable, obvious: If people had not had it in for me, I would have been much more successful. During one period when I was a youngster, I engaged in petty thievery. At times, I feel like smashing things.

We were gaunt in appearance, had enlarged pupils, reacted in slo-mo, were slow to understand, slow to grasp, slow at everything, clinically anxious, depressed, bipolar, suicidal, certifiable. Occasionally, the police or FBI came and arrested someone. And though we were dumb, thoughtless, and lacking foresight, we were genius, old school, streetwise. How could we respond to questions that came from both nowhere and deep inside? It seemed our hearts had broken loose and were laid out now on paper: I've had periods of days, weeks, or months when I couldn't take care of things because I couldn't get it going. My sleep is fitful and disturbed. I don't always tell the truth. My soul sometimes leaves my body.

I wanted to insert parentheticals, exclamation points,

comments on syntax, word choice. It evoked feelings of mistrust, confusion: I prefer to pass by school friends, or people I know but have not seen in a long time, unless they speak to me first. I am liked by most people who know me. Even when clear-cut, true/false was too confining: As a youngster, I was suspended from school one or more times for cutting up. Where do I write my "yes, but"? I wanted third and fourth options to rebut, justify, evoke meaning: I am a good mixer. The *fuck* does it mean: I have not lived a good life. Parts of my body often have feelings like burning, tingling, crawling, or "going to sleep." I sometimes keep on at a thing until others lose patience with me.

We asked why, what for, and, waiting, heard pencils snap, erasers scrub: I get angry sometimes. I am troubled by discomfort in the pit of my stomach every few days or oftener. I am an important person. I wish I could be as happy as others seem to be. I enjoy reading love stories. I like poetry. Most of the time I feel blue. I think I would like the kind of work a forest ranger does. I am easily downed in an argument. I would like to be a florist. I usually feel that life is worthwhile. It takes a lot in an argument to convince most people of the truth. Once in a while I put off until tomorrow what I ought to do today.

The questions cycled on with slight word changes, phrasing flipped. Inverses. I'd like to be a nurse. Most people would lie to get ahead. Dirt is nice, etc. I do many things I regret afterward. I was suspended from school one or more times for bad behavior. At times, I have a strong urge to do something harmful or shocking. I have met problems so full of possibilities that I have been unable to make up my mind about them. My hardest battles are with myself. I don't seem to care what happens to me. I love my father. Or, if my father is dead, I loved my father.

EVERY FEW WEEKS a group of boys' families came, and then those boys went into the wilderness for three weeks on Trip. Trip was supposed to be a coming-of-age moment, meant to foster faith and lay a foundation of self-belief, and indeed boys returned so moved by the experience their feet never hit the ground and they'd hover about mess and regale us with one half-told tale or another—I'd tell you more, they'd explain, but you had to be there. And though boys *were* changed by the event—they listened intently now, laughed harder, gave less a fuck but less a fuck in a good way—I had zero expectations for Trip and no hope beyond survival.

When word came that my pot-filled boots had arrived, a tech pulled me from the rumpus, escorted me to the rancher's home. I thought for sure I'd be kicked out now. But inside that warm home, the tech just laughed at me, pointed at my empty boots. Nice one. Try again. Better luck next time.

Fuck. I untied my shoes and pulled the boots on. That it?

No. He pointed at the phone. Your mom wants to talk.

Okay, I thought, okay. Here comes the noise. She'd gripe about what a manipulative "jerk" I was, but silt clogged her voice, all throaty and sad. Sweetie, she said, I know you don't want to talk about your dad, but—

I cut her off. I don't.

—I've been having this feeling.

Leave it, Mom.

I called your grampa. How are things, by the way?

What did Grampa say?

Oh, sweetie, she said. You know. He loves your dad very much. He. He's sad.

About what?

You need to call your dad. He's expecting you. I love you.

I hung up and watched the tech zip his coat and then unzip it. The rancher came in. His wife, too. She was a small woman whom we rarely saw, and she sat at the edge of a chair and looked at me. Well, she said.

I'll call him.

She nodded. The tech nodded. The rancher stared at the floor. They all knew.

I guess I joked with my dad at first. You'll never guess where I am—ha-ha.

I know where you are, he said.

You talked to my mom?

I know where you are.

So, yeah. Well. That's how the story ends, anyway. No college.

You don't know that.

I know I won't be going to Harvard.

Whatever, he said. That place is a shithole.

It's been weird, Dad, I said. Very. And I wanted to tell him things, mostly about sports, how much they meant to me. I thought this was about me. He'd be curious. We were reconnected; we'd start over. I told him about Drake, cited their home record, described being down late on the road and rallying, how clutch I was, the crowd, how I couldn't hear anything anymore, and I wanted to tell him something about something else, something equally important about something I was sure he'd want to know, but—

Listen, he said. I have some news.

Tell me, I said.

He told me. He had AIDS.

What does that mean? I asked.

It means what you think it means.

How long have you had it?

Since 1980 or '82, he said. Full-blown since '87. You're not in any danger, if that's what you're thinking. Son? What are you thinking?

I don't know.

Do you have any questions for me?

I could think of a few, but they all seemed mean now and petty.

You can ask me anything you want, he said.

And then I understood he wanted me to ask the kinds of questions people ask when you offer them news like this, but I didn't know those kinds of questions.

Son, he said. Do you know anything about it?

I know about Magic Johnson, I said. People die. Everyone dies, right? You don't recover from it, right? It's terminal?

First you're positive. You can live positive. I've lived a long time positive. A long, long time. When you start losing T cells, you get the disease. Run out of T cells and you die.

How many T cells do you have left?

Less than twenty.

What does that mean?

It means what I said.

You're going to die?

Yes.

How long do you have?

A few months. Maybe less.

A few months.

Maybe less.

And?

Son, he said. I've lived a good life. I'm okay with it. I have no regrets. Not one.

WHAT HAPPENS IN THESE PLACES is you get very good at Ping-Pong and blowing O-rings. There's a vernacular to a treatment center, we called it TC talk; we're all well versed in it by now. Alone time was rare, efficiency critical: we could all beat off in less than a minute. We war-storied about drugs and booze, sex, money, violence; 95 percent of it was spot-on bullshit, and yet all of it was 100 percent true. Almost no one talked about being salutatorian or testing in the ninety-ninth percentile on the Iowa Test of Basic What-have-you. No one bragged on their parents' hopes anymore or described the long-ago dreams of taking over the family business or running for political office one day. Our former potential was shameful now. I grew watchful, studious: how could I get out of here? I worked the steps they gave me. I learned things. On the outside, cool meant a fast car, expensive shades, a hot chick, a dope fade, but in here it meant appraising a situation before it could appraise you.

Fuck it. If I talked, maybe they'd let me out. So I talked. I cried. I wrung my hands. A strange thing happened. I began sleeping better. Quickly, from shared misery and parallel existences, relationships developed so thickly bonded I felt sure I'd know these boys forever; we made plans on the outs to drop acid in the Angeles, Joshua Tree, Half Dome, and in the rocks above the Yuba, or some guy had a brother whose girlfriend's best friend's boyfriend had an ethereal connect for sheets, elbows, and vials of the purest meth in the entire central San Joaquin. But true to this thing's nature, the child actor disappeared within a week of my arrival, and most the other boys left soon after.

For now I reveled in that feel-sorry-for-me muck, expecting everyone else to do so as well. Oh, hey, I thought they'd say, never mind. The dude has every reason. He's right. No one's ever loved him. Let's give him a break. He's clearly different. And yet the night after revealing my father's illness, I woke up with shaving cream coating my face and the young boy spastically dancing about. In the bathroom, while cleaning myself, I considered beating him senseless. But can you beat someone who doesn't care about pain? No. You have to kill them. I searched for some dental floss to pull through his throat, but there was none. Outside I lit a cigarette, stared at the sky. Here were stars on top of stars on top of stars, all backlit by numerous galaxies. Is that a bear? Is it a hunter hunting a bear? What was I thinking? Would guillotining this fool further my goals? *No.* From then on, whenever he came skulking along, pockets full of rocks and shit to throw, I'd simply open a pack of cigarettes and offer whatever. Here's a dollar or fifty cents. Here's a pen, it's all I've got. Want my sandwich? A hat? Are you tired? Can I rub your feet?

He terrified me, but in their own way, they all did.

I HEARD VISALIA shouting in the woods, and then he emerged from a stand of birch holding a large femur above his head.

He claimed it came from Sasquatch and dandied about the group, showing it off. One boy took it and shook his head. This here, he informed us, is a cow's bone.

Visalia grabbed it back. You don't know dick, he said. Holding the bone between his biceps and lat, he removed a drawstring from his hoodie and tied the bone at both ends, draping it around his neck.

It was Christmas Day, 1994.

There are many photographs of us, all slender-faced and hollow-eyed boys with scruffy necks and chins, our eyes obscured by dangling hair. In most I'm wearing snow boots, jeans, and a field jacket. I can't see my thermals, though I know I'm wearing them. The photos are relics taken with disposable point-and-click cameras, all of them overexposed. We are always smoking, our arms draped around each other's shoulders, hanging from one another as if, were we to let go, we would fall.

Written inside my Big Book are many notes and letters, like a high school yearbook. There are addresses, phone numbers, signatures, promises—Yo, it's been fun. We'll be killing some caps this summer. I'm going to miss you. I'll write. Write me. I'll write you back—but we were all just travelers, and like most travelers, we'd slide past one another eventually. I don't know what happened to most of the boys. The kid? Shit. No idea. Visalia jumped off a roof and is dead.

A FEW YEARS LATER, I was living in Los Angeles with this girl. I was bone-dry then, very close to not existing. We lived in a mid-rise on top of a hill, and each night I'd climb the ten flights of stairs and stand on our roof's edge, imagining a free fall into nothing. I'd gone crazy, I guess, and wanted to die.

I decided to track down the child actor, see if he could give me some of his old enthusiasm. It was a very hush-hush operation, I recall, very cloak-and-dagger, as if he were Leo DiCaprio now—I'd call one Westside number and leave a message, and he'd call back from another number two days later, leave word of some kind, Call me at this other place, this guy's house, let it ring a few times, hang up, call back immediately. And would I meet him somewhere, like Lincoln and Rose?

He wasn't doing well. Truly, he'd found a new worseness. He was homeless or thereabouts, sleeping in one man's bed or another, banging dope. The same old same.

A year later, someone told me he'd passed.

Almost all of us—but not all—are dead now.

I find myself googling the dead ones again and again. Will anything change? Will any new information come to light? For years, on IMDb and Rotten Tomatoes, the child actor's name offered an avatar with only a question mark, a few dreary day-player credits, nothing remarkable. But then one day I looked once more, and his avatar had changed. In place of the question mark was a photo of a middle-aged man who'd grown his locks out into a manbun. Gone now his fancy mountain beard; he wore some real Hollywood stubble. His bio listed a wife, some kids. He was alive.

Lessons

At six weeks sober, I had no memory of my mom's house. Couldn't tell you a thing about her living room, kitchen, or dining area, didn't know where her TV was, if she even owned one, or what pictures hung on her walls. I learned other things. Terrible things. Boys, when they left here, did not go home. Instead they went to far-flung Omaha or Crapsville, Louisiana. No one wanted to go there. Louisiana was scary. We heard stories about it, true shit: counselors beat you there; they literally whaled on you. But, guys said, you can get a GED. You have some freedom. Still, I was skeptical.

Wind kept whipping down from the mountains, blowing the crystalline snow. After Christmas came the New Year. Goodbye, 1994. I'd been speaking to my dad for a few weeks now, always ending with the same report—a few months to go. Knowing him became my number one thing, and I called when they let me, asked all the things a young man will ask the father he never knew, said like Tell me how great you are, and then he'd tell me, or I'd ask how smart he was and he'd say, Very, very smart, son, and I'd call him Dad and prompt him in ways that excused his behavior and explained why he wasn't around.

Do you think, I'd say, you were always afraid of getting close because you loved me so fucking much? Oh, yes, he'd say. That's it. It's exactly what it was.

In the afternoons, our dyadic encounters and paperwork done, me and the rez kids scraped ice off a slab of concrete and got burn on the slippery half-court. I was still dunking and doing so with ferocity. But I wasn't the only one. The court had a bent rim, its net a tangled mass of frozen chains, and we played one-on-one, two-on-two or two-on-three, twenty-one, Utahs, and fifty, always all-out, hateful, our shoulders dipped, crown bowed, swinging wildly. One day the court disappeared under snow too high to shovel, and we handlessly smoked while playing bloody knuckles. This was painful, but the pain was easy to understand. My knuckles swelled up and burst. Barely able to close my fist, I kept swinging. A social worker came hauling ass through the snow.

What are y'all doing? he asked, pulling us apart. What's going on here? This is not the place. It's not how we do things here.

Why are you so surprised? I asked, but he didn't answer. He just glared at me, eyes cold and full of shame, until I looked away.

Later, on the porch, I eyed the prairie and mountains. The setting sun cast a lingering glow, shading the snow a dim pink. I tugged at my beard, swept the bangs off my face. My hair was so long I could chew it in my mouth.

THEY MOVED ME OUT of the big cabin and into a small one where I lived with just one other boy, Donald. He never spoke.

Not in group or mess, not in the rumpus or on the prairie while we dug rocks. He didn't talk about his past, didn't bitch about the tests or work, didn't war-story, didn't joke. He never said a word.

He was from a notoriously rough reservation in a forgotten part of the state, a place beyond hardscrabble, beyond marginalized, where pipes freeze and pickup trucks never run and all the homes are missing floorboards and doors, where children are stolen and sold by Russians and every male over a certain age is in fact the bogeyman. Donald was just about that age and knew it. He had close inset eyes, a scumstash. A scar covered one of his cheeks—he'd taken a bottle there once. He wore a Raiders parka, jeans, and high-top sneakers, but never gloves or a hat, never earmuffs or a scarf. He was like, Oh, is it cold? So. Fucking. What. I don't care. He had a rattail, mean streaks razored into each eyebrow and above his ears. He'd stand on the porch huffing into his bare fists, the shittiness of his seventeen years replaying in the snowy limbs of evergreens as he rocked back and forth on his heels, or he'd sit on the weight bench or in group, his arms crossed, always that same stoic far-off look on his face. Tough, but not boastful, his grit exposed itself only in silence: life is this, so what.

He would not be my friend.

MY FAMILY CAME. Not my dad, of course, or Aidan, but Abba, my mom, Lee. I think I was talking about going home. And where is that? my mom asked.

But I couldn't answer her—not directly, only hint. Huh? I asked.

Sixteen is old enough, she said, and you are seventeen.

She sat perched at the edge of a chair, tissue balled in her fist, unblinking and unsmiling. I had to consider this. All around me, winter had been growing more defined in its principles—colder, darker, less sun, more ice—and here was this coldness beyond all that, a coldness that wouldn't stop.

Then Lee told everyone how I tried to kill him that time with the baseball bat.

I guess it's true. It's hard to judge intent. I remember the moment, though. I'll take his word for it.

Of course, in some places this kind of information would have made me unsavory, but not here. Here it impressed people. Suddenly, I was much cooler than before. That motherfucker tried to kill someone, people said. And that is *always* cool. Killing someone isn't cool, obviously, but trying to shows something.

I tossed and turned that night, trying to conceive a new plan. I could ask my dad to take me in, or traffic dirt weed, maybe find work in a warehouse. Long detailed blow-by-blows kept me awake, all of them heroic, as if I were Robinson Crusoe.

Donald started laughing.

I knew he was laughing at me. Nothing else could be so funny. What? I said.

I thought you were some pussy, he said. Not a damn killer.

Well, I said. He's still alive, isn't he?

Huh, he said. No shit.

That's right, I told him.

He asked for a cigarette and I handed him one, and though smoking wasn't allowed inside, neither of us cared. Who knows how we conveyed the unspoken? Is it like when vampires spot each other? Is it born of instinct, the commonality of bloodlust, or just the wisdom of living eight hundred years? Or, like snakes who den together, how it doesn't matter their breed, whether they're viper or constrictor, garter or king, they will all climb the same hill and all crawl to the same damn hollow—thousands of them, sometimes more—where they'll tangle together in one giant denning ball of scale and fang and spit.

You know what, Donald said. Fuck it. I'ma tell you something.

She'd lived in Yakima, where Donald had family. They'd met at fourteen, fallen in love, he'd been young—this was a long time ago, he explained, a long, long time—and in and out of school, already gangster, banging with heavy hitters, future hard-timers, real fucked-up dudes, so this here, with her, was different, strange—Can I say, he asked, can I tell you this? He visited her as often as possible, took buses, hitchhiked, caught rides with uncles and aunts, truckers, whoever. As he spoke, I imagined the loneliness of those rides, how quiet they must have been, always needle at ninety, hell-bent under that big sky, his heart beating with love, hurtling toward elusive mountains on a horizon he'd never reach. Nothing in his life had ever made the kind of sense life is supposed to make. He'd known brutality instead, rage, ugliness, pain; he knew the price of Mad Dog and could tell by the weight of his jeans if he had the coins to meet that price or could only afford a shorty; what mattered to him were cigarettes, a shipment of brick weed, how many .22s he had left, how to pack a slug or turkey-bag dope, and how to, yeah, take a motherfucker out if need be, but he'd never known anything as sweet as holding this girl. At the end of the day—she'd be there. He dropped his guard, then lost it, got vulnerable, let things go, so instead of imagining trouble around the next bend, he imagined her and this thing they had, this beauty, lifting him higher and higher. In train or bus station, next to stranger or family, in cab or truck bed, standing along a highway's edge, he thought of her. One day, crossing Idaho, he decided that when he got back to the rez, he'd sell a sheet of acid, buy a truck, and move to Yakima for good, and so he procured and sold the shit and found an old Silverado owned in part by an uncle who sold it to him for a few hundred bucks, and what he thought, filling its tank with gasoline, and stuffing the cab with his parka, clothes, loose change, cigarettes, shotgun shells and sawed-off, was that life would be good. The drive took no more than thirty minutes. He flew, sailed, even *skyrocketed* west, imagining beginnings and endings, dawns, good nights, and a place to come home to, but when he got to his girl's mom's place, she wasn't home. He asked a neighbor, but the neighbor didn't know shit, and so he asked another neighbor who pointed to a house where maybe the girl's uncle lived, but the uncle wasn't home, he was shooting pool, a woman at the door said, laughing, but her cousin, who was *definitely* shooting pool, might know something. At the pool hall this cousin said no, but he knew this bad motherfucker named Rudolph who lived in a trailer park near the hop fields, but when Donald went there, he couldn't find Rudolph or anyone willing to admit they knew or had heard of any Rudolph, and so he returned to the billiards place, where he saw a blood cousin of his own who said, Hell yes, saw that bitch earlier, kicking it with a guy Harlan off North First, but on North First he saw only the usual bellyachers rolling on the curb or slumped against walls, bandanas hanging from pockets, a sad western light edging the steely gray sky. And does anyone know Harlan or my girl, he asked up and down North First, until a guy pulled his head from his chest, wiped his eyes of sleep, and said, That fuck's at the movies with his girl, he likes movies, they both like movies, everybody likes movies, and so Donald went back to his truck, loaded up his shotgun, and set out for the movie theater.

Sometimes there isn't anything to do but stop listening, even when a story continues; all you can hear is wind rattling the windows, the flick of your Zippo, a crackling cigarette. Whatever he said now wasn't for my ears—only the telling mattered, and only to him.

We grew inseparable.

Bullies

We prepped for weeks, learned how to build snow caves, igloos, lean-tos. We skied. A lot. Like every day. After group, before diagnostics. Up and down the hills surrounding the ranch, across fields, for miles on end. We dried fruits and meats, made granola bars, gorp, high-protein bombs we'd eat for lunch. We took classes, how-to and survival. We participated in rope courses. We got fit.

In the preparation, certain things grew clear. I'd be on Trip when baseball season began. Possibly while I was out there, my dad would die. What happened now would determine my next residence. A lot of boys got sent to adult facilities, places where they had to grow up. This meant no school, no baseball. Other things—it was winter and cold. Nicotine and caffeine restrict circulation; they'd be off-limits. We'd be skiing in big-game country. We discussed bears often. In the winter, when it's unseasonably warm, bears emerge from dens looking to eat and screw. This was important. A bear, it's known, will fuck a human if it wants to. They are animals, and animals don't care.

We discussed hypothermia, knew full well the problem of hypothermia—it doesn't take much; all you got to do is get wet. You can die from it at fifty degrees. We talked frostbite, told stories of boys who got frostbite, lost their fingers and toes, had them shits chopped right off. We talked spruce traps, tree wells, deep voids, hollows, black holes in snow that will snag and bury you. We talked about what to do in case of emergency, if we got lost or separated, how to proceed and act.

The first week in the wilderness, we awoke each day at four a.m., skied up and down heavily wooded hills all day, and were asleep by six p.m. These were long days. We wore long underwear, sock liners, wool socks, rubber pants, water- and windproof nylons over everything. We wore Sorels, gaiters, base layers and wicking layers, big parkas, headgear like astronauts. We carried sixty-pound packs and dragged ninety-pound sleds loaded down with tents, sleeping bags, pots, pans, sternos, and nine dinners and nine breakfasts for nine people. On the tenth day, we planned to resupply. We also carried bags of lunch stuff—the dried meats and protein what-have-you—for which there was no resupply. What you made at the ranch and brought to the woods was it. Meting out our lunch stuff was important. We needed to ski ten or more miles each day. Calories were essential.

Nine of us went out there—seven boys, a wilderness guide, and a social worker—and though nine of us returned, what does it really mean to come back? You are here and you are there. Parts of us emerge only in certain places, like when shrouded, how only in total darkness can we find light, or only from badness goodness is born, and sometimes lines blur,

there're no heroes, no guilt, just what happened. I'm thinking of the peppy-stepped guide, who had a Ph.D. in outdoor
adventure and for whom this was a dream job, who every day
bubbled with optimism and joy, a smile gleaming in his frosty
beard, who, after this, quit working at the home; and the social
worker. Ours was the first time the home sent a woman on
Trip. It was also the last.

LANKY AND FIT, magical on a pair of skis, the guide swished
about in perfect form. I know fuck-all about winter sports but
have long legs and an earnest desire for pain. Plus, I'm a real
bonehead when it comes to giving up. My motto is Fuck You.
I can ski all day. We had two Jeffs on Trip. Good Jeff skied
pretty, swanlike and graceful. Bad Jeff was passable, athletic;
he could move. Big Bill, who was older and had recently been
kicked out of the navy, had long strides, and watch out should
his big ass get behind you on a downhill—that fucker could
fly. Donald, Kev, and Shawn were all okay. No one was mistaking them for Greg Louganis or whoever, but they did well in
effort categories. All of us were okay except the social worker.
Her brain sent the wrong messages to her body. She lacked
athleticism, possessed no endurance, and skied slower and
slower each passing day. Even fastening her backpack troubled
her. It hung loose about her body, all awkward and wanting.
Often she stopped. Often she removed her backpack. Often
she rested, looking at her pack. She always refastened it exactly
the same way.

Planned ten-mile treks became eight, and we fell behind
resupply. We found ourselves many afternoons in the middle

of some wooded trail, nowhere near water, and miles from our intended camp, knowing, in the waning light, we had to stop. We consumed fewer calories; tempers flared.

I felt bad. Truly. The social worker was pitiful, out of place. I wanted to help, but helping meant correcting, and she was not the type of person you correct.

No-no, she'd say, personal responsibility, accountability, and so forth. Or she'd get hysterical about "macho posturing," "blah-blah," "out here," "in the wild." She was an illustrator or writer on the side, and she'd look at us with her sad writer eyes and predict all our tomorrows by how we behaved today. She'd thaw her finger over the fire just to shake it in our faces. You'll use again, she'd say, and you and you, and you I'm not so sure of, but you and you and you, too.

We'd ask, Just what do you expect of us? and she'd say, For you to work a program, and we'd say, We're trying, and she'd start up with that TC talk—trying's dying—get all Yoda. Try to pick up that rock, she'd say. Go on. No. I didn't say pick it up. I said *try*. You either do or don't. You either are or aren't.

Maybe this kind of talk makes sense in a warm prefab, but out here, making camp before dark meant life or death. She began pulling nonsense. Now, when she stopped to unfasten her bag, she'd unpack it, repack it the same way, stop thirty minutes later to repeat, always the same—lightest gear on bottom, heaviest on top—creating a cycle of irritation, forcing our tempo, slowing it, always blah-blah, you dick-slingers, you cowboys, you misogynists; I don't need your fucking help.

She wasn't dumb, we knew, but stupid in that way smart people are stupid for thinking they're outsmarting someone so clearly beneath them.

We shifted her within our line front to back and back to front, putting our fastest on her heels to harry her, and talked incessantly, we all did: C'mon, now, push, push, you can do it, push.

Enough, she said. It doesn't matter how fast I ski. In the world, y'all don't matter and I do. In two weeks, you'll be using and I'll still be sober. Two years from now, you'll be dead and I'll be sipping hot chocolate someplace warm.

I WANTED TO KEEP MY HEAD DOWN. If I kept my head down, maybe they'd let me go home. So I skied. I watched the others. I made camp, helped cook and clean, slept, broke camp, skied again the next day. Sleep came easy. I don't know what pushed the others, if they thought they were going home, if they even wanted to. I'm sure at the time I knew exactly what everyone believed for themselves—both their hopes as children and their revised dreams. Maybe they, too, had simply moved on to the practical.

I can recall us being honest with one another, yet only in that way the young are honest. Tent flaps open under a billion stars, we talked about the ways we'd be better. Or how a hope will flatline. And we'd ask, Is that flat line a good thing or bad? Of course we discussed other things, too. Our bathroom habits. Our wilderdumps. How much snow was enough snow to roll in the handfuls of Spanish moss we used to wipe our ass. And girls. Always girls. Ones we knew, would know, or wished we knew, but always the social worker came over the top, batty and defensive—Watch your language, be respectful, shut it—and one night I said something back and she said, Here he goes with his mouth again. He'll be the first to tell you how smart he is. HA! Let me tell you what he scored on his MMPI. He has, she said, the mind of a small child, a boy. He's dumb. He doesn't know anything.

About that MMPI, I scoffed.

It is what it is, she said. You're dumb. I didn't take the test. They're your scores.

And what could I say to this? For all I knew, she was right.

Your dad is dying, she said. How do you feel about that?

Boys quieted themselves around the fire. No one moved. Not even me. I had no idea how to answer that question.

If you want to see him again, she warned, you'll behave.

The wilderness guide was a normie and wasn't supposed to get involved, wasn't supposed to talk about recovery, life, or anything. He had one job and one job only: lead us safely through the mountains.

He stared into the fire, an impossible stillness to his small mouth.

I FOUND MYSELF miles ahead of the group, all alone, really, and happy, when I came across a heap of steaming shit on the trail; bear or mountain lion scat, I'm no expert. It scared me silly. The day was balmy, bright, maybe forty degrees, and this sense of the unseasonably warm brought unease. That night some of the boys found a bottle of hooch in the woods and drank. I don't remember who. It wouldn't matter, I guess, if I did. It wasn't me. But even that doesn't matter. We were all going to drink again eventually. In that way, the social worker was right and we were wrong.

OUR PLANS THE NEXT DAY called for making camp in a valley for two nights and climbing one of the mountains. This climb was important, we were told, both before coming out here and again now. Things will change for you on that mountain, the social worker said. She instructed us to gather rocks and fill our pockets with them. A lot of them. These rocks, she told us, are your past and your resentments. You'll climb the mountain carrying these rocks and, at the top of the mountain, release them to the elements. You could say you'll be letting go or whatever. It's a metaphor, she explained.

Seemed dumb to me. Ditto the others. No one wanted to climb a mountain. Our camp sat in a quiet valley of birch and evergreen. Alongside our bivouac of pup tents and snow caves, a river was frozen at its rapids, wavy and white and pure.

It was warm again. Eerily so.

Won't need your parkas, gentlemen, the guide said. Just lunch stuff, water, your windbreakers. It'll be warm on trail, you'll sweat. He marched about in trim pants and an ascot. We're going straight up, he said, and straight down. Be on trail eight hours, tops.

It was late already, past ten a.m. What the shit? guys asked. How we fixing to try? No way we summit and return before sundown.

Why not, the social worker said.

We wanted to tell her the truth—it was because of her, she hadn't trained, hadn't skied in years, and wasn't in shape—but shut our mouths. Of course, sometimes when you shut your mouth and stare blankly into a fire or busy yourself with chores no one wants to do, like the scullery, you are saying quite a lot.

She frowned. She stomped her feet and grabbed at her ears, peacocking about and peering into our eyes. She detected some feelings, she said. She wanted to have group.

No time for group, we said. Not if we're fixing to climb.

The guide remained passive, his sunglasses reflecting the sky above, and yet she insisted. Always time for group, she said. I'll start.

She felt bullied. Controlled. She'd come out here expecting some fun in the snow, but this wasn't fun. Not at all. Being rushed isn't fun. Normally, she loved skiing and was a good skier, but we'd sapped her of its joy. It was our fault. We had bad attitudes. We made her a worse skier. Because we were mean. No one likes being told how fast to move! It's human nature, she explained. Ask anyone!

We all said yup, you're right, my bad, but no, sir, she did *not* feel heard and continued rambling for another hour or two. This and that. Blah-blah. You and you and you. While she spoke, the guide stuffed his daypack with the coiled rope that mountaineers tie around their skis for icy inclines, but by the end of her speech, he'd looped a rope around a low-hanging branch and was tying a noose around his throat. Boys had to be kicked awake. Big Bill foamed at the mouth. Shawn bled from his ears.

At noon, four hours till sundown, we set out.

*   *   *

AND WHAT DO YOU DO when your pity runs out? How do you behave when things shift? How do you treat someone who once lorded their might over you once things have turned and you occupy the high ground? Are you kind? Are you forgiving? Or do you bully?

We fucked with the woman that afternoon, stopping every few minutes, claiming we had to piss or lay cable, all of it tom-foolery, grab-ass, slap and tickle, mocking her—we'd crest a hill and remove our rocks, toss them in the snow. Here's as good a place as any.

It drove her insane. If any of you stop again, she claimed, I'll make your next home unimaginable. It'll set you back ten years. They'll make you get your GED, and you'll fade into a cycle of middle management at a fast-food company, if you're lucky. Go on, she said. Pee again, Tommy boy, and kiss your college dreams goodbye.

We picked up handfuls of snow and jiggled our wrists, here's a handful, whatever.

You little, she shrieked. You little pieces of. As if a loon. Louder and louder. Her voice rolled through the lows and boomeranged again and again. Her shrieking became too much and we climbed. At first densely packed with fir and spruce, once we got higher, the trees thinned. At eight thousand feet, they took on odd forms: shorter, squatter, now their needles grew only downwind.

The sun fell.

Snow turned to ice.

We wrapped ropes around our skis and waists. The

switchbacks narrowed, tightened, the trail steepened. No longer perpendicular, we inched on, parallel to the mountain. Coming around one bend, I saw the contours of a frozen lake thousands of feet below, but on the switchback, its contours faded, and the valley floor finally disappeared altogether.

Summiting felt only like stopping, another break—a place to pick at the last few oats collecting in the corner of my food bag. I was hungry, uncomfortable. Somewhere in front of us, the mountain's edge led to a ten-thousand-foot free fall, but a lowering cloud front blocked the moon and stars, and all I saw was a black nothing. I knew, because Donald told me, in the mythical distance lay Canada.

In the daytime, he said, you can see the fucking North Pole.

Ain't that some shit. I can't even see the edge of this mountain.

Oh yeah, he told me. We're going to die up here.

Is that true? I asked.

He produced a few rocks and tossed them on the ground. Say your prayers, man.

I turned to the guide. What now?

Well, there's no way we can ski back down that way, he said. Too much ice. No big deal. We'll just ski down the back side.

Have you done this before?

No, he admitted. I've never been here in my life.

So you don't know what's on the back side. Am I right?

He didn't respond. Not really. Just insisted, It'll be okay. Take a few hours, he said. Tops. We'll be back in camp by midnight. At most.

It was six p.m.

*　　*　　*

I DON'T KNOW if you've ever seen those movies where mother-fuckers get lost in the woods. It's always cold, the lenses drip with rain, sleet, and snow. The actors want you to think, because they're told to act this way, they're hungry and tired. And maybe they are. Filming requires long hours—chances are some of their feelings are real. They probably don't like each other much, even when they're playing buddies. They smell bad, their hair's greasy. Often a bear shows up, or a mountain lion, maybe a pit viper, and one of these players gets eaten ass through belly. If you've seen one of those pictures, then you might understand the feelings we had. They weren't good. Boys were scared. The social worker was scared. Even the guide seemed rattled.

Ten hours passed. We were still on the mountain. Ten hours. Still sloshing along. Every so often we called out to the guide. Hey, you. Up there. Are we lost?

Nope. He knew our exact location—still on the mountain!

Yes, but are we lost?

Silence.

One dumb, stupid thing about me, though: the closer I come to calamity, the calmer I feel. I just kept skiing under the canopy of pines, listening to the prattle on prattle on of boys who don't want to sound scared. It's a fucked-up thing to know this boisterousness for what it is and then—in one moment—have it fade away to the swoosh-swoosh of skis and the semi-silence of group fear.

I don't remember who broke first, but once it happened, everyone burst open. Boys called to the low sky and trees. They called at the snow and one another, fell to their stomachs and cursed, punched the snowpack and pines. I kept an eye out for

Bad Jeff, the type of boy who will act as good or bad as those around him. Put a gun in his hand and tell him to shoot a guy in the back and he will pull the trigger. Yet in the end it was Good Jeff who snapped.

Good Jeff was mild-mannered, unwavering, friendly, empathetic. He'd talk about anything. Whatever troubled you, he cared. How are you? he'd ask. Need a hug, an ear? Scars lined his wrists along his radial artery. He'd downed a hundred sleeping pills once, swallowed two hundred Advils, hung himself from a rafter, jumped off a bridge, but survived. He was a walking advertisement, a true miracle. This is what happens, the child actor had said, you stay down this road: Shit gets worse and then worse still. You reach a point of sobriety or death. It's anything but this. And Good Jeff had got there. He was done. Going to make it or die. He never bitched about the social worker or being in the home, never bemoaned the left-behind world. He wanted to be here. And yet now, lost in the woods on a dark mountain, thirty miles out with no food or shelter, no flashlight, no matches, or winter coat, tired and scared, a new sense of things emerged. He knew once and for all, after so many attempts, he would die. This was it. He was going to die sober. He sat down in the snow, removed his skis, and refused to go on.

I yelled for the others to hold up.

The social worker screamed. What did I say? No more stopping. Hello? Jeff? Get. Up.

He needs a minute, I told her, though clearly, he needed more than a minute. I crouched beside him. My friend, I said. Man? Can you make it?

No, he said. I'm done.

He needs to collect himself, I said.

He clutched at me, shaking his head. I've never been so clearheaded in my life. Please, he begged, leave me. It's over.

I reached out for his arm, saying how much I admired and needed him, but the social worker came stomping through the snow, falling as she did, righting herself, marching on, until she grabbed at my windbreaker and pulled me free of Jeff. Get the fuck away from him. Her breath reeked of bile, malnourishment, dehydration.

Why, Good Jeff asked, are you yelling at him?

Get up, she screamed. GET UP!

So he got up. And in her face. Just kick me right in the dick, he growled, if that's what you want. He yanked off his pants and long underwear, exposing a cold penis and some constricted balls, which he clutched at. Kick me right in the nuts, why don't you. Go on, if it makes you feel better. He flipped dick-down in the snow and began squirting about as if a penguin. And then—I don't know—he must have skidded over a spruce trap. A branch snapped. He disappeared into the powdery nothing.

ALL I CAN SPEAK TO now are outcomes. Both Jeffs would eventually smoke rock again and disappear into correctional cycles, etc. Big Bill returned home to work for his family, but they fired him. Shawn went to a facility in Omaha, then moved in with his mother, where he stayed sober a while, working in kitchens, attending college, and drumming in a band, until finally, he disappeared. Kev never made it home. As for myself, well, this was twenty years ago, and as bleak as things seemed then, they were not bleak, for I didn't know who I was yet and, in the unknowing, still had a lot to look forward to. I thought I'd go back to school, to college eventually, find a career, a girl, have a home. Maybe not right away but someday.

The guide quit his job. The social worker never went on another trip. And I was not going home.

THE FOLLOWING DAY, after we'd returned to camp safely and regrouped, while the guide and social worker tried to make sense of what had happened on the mountain, Donald and I followed the frozen river into a stand of birches, and he asked me, he said, Hey, what do you think, should we go back to camp, pull the social worker from her tent, drag her ass out here, and rape her?

I wasn't sure if he was serious or speaking in some weirdly negative euphemism.

You know what'll happen, he said, if we don't.

We were supposed to ski twenty-two miles the following day, a double day, really, to make up for the lost time, to resupply for the trek out of the wilderness. It was a hard, flat number— impossible to imagine. By my own calculations, including the variables of energy, mood, and the social worker's laziness, I believed it would take twenty hours.

I shook my head. It's hard to say, really.

From the birch, I could see downriver to our scattered camp of tents, snow caves, and gear. The sun had just slipped behind the mountain, and the gloaming cast a dimness across the snow. Shawn and Kev stood above the water on its shore. Below them, leaning over the icy crust, Big Bill held a large rock above his head. He seemed to be entertaining some private thoughts, though I hadn't slept yet—none of us had—and the severity of his thoughts didn't register. I felt dreamlike, vague, as if watching something in slow motion I'd seen already.

Smoke fluttered from the fire where Good Jeff was warming himself. Something stirred in the treeline. The wilderness guide emerged from the woods, a smile in his beard. I couldn't see the social worker.

It's a true thing that any time two boys huddle in a place like this, they're either confiding or conspiring. Bad Jeff sloshed over and asked which was it.

Donald gave him a look like what do you think.

I'm in, Bad Jeff said. Whatever it is.

That makes two, Donald told me.

I shook my head.

C'mon, Tommy, Donald said. This is bullshit, man. I need some pussy.

Look, I get sometimes things are about needing some pussy, I've been there, but this wasn't about needing pussy, and even a dumb virgin knew that. This was a statement of fact: I am bigger, stronger, and more powerful than you can imagine; I will hold you down and become your fear because I hate you and I can.

What do you think? Donald asked.

Ask me tomorrow.

Do it tomorrow?

Ask me tomorrow.

Tomorrow?

We'll talk about it tomorrow.

*   *   *

WHEN TOMORROW CAME, we squatted about the remains of
the fire, all of us eyeing one another, asking: Are you ready?
Can you keep yourself together? We'd be skiing in the dark
again today, we'd be hungry, we'd be tired, and uncertain.
Donald shook his head at me and frowned at the social worker,
who stood off to the side, slumped and disheveled, her baggy
parka unzipped and flapping in the wind, her backpack on
but unfastened. Behind her, tied to her waist, was a sled. No,
I thought, no-no, no-fucking-no, yeah-nope, not happening.

Listen, I started to say, and I meant to give her a kind of
tough-love talk about limits and self-realization and humility,
only I was planning on being much more curt about it, something like Get your head out of your ass, or even Get serious,
but the wilderness guide jumped to his feet.

What the fuck is he doing? he said.

Big Bill was out in the middle of the frozen river, knees
bent, struggling to gain balance. He was holding a shovel.
Once steady, he raised the shovel above his head and smashed
it into the ice. He lifted it again and smacked the ice once
more. He stabbed the spade into the crusty rapids and kicked
it. He was methodical, earnest; he kicked again and again
until the shovel broke though. He worked the handle back
and forth, snapping the ice. Then he sat down, removed his
boots and socks, flung them to the shore, rolled back his
rubber pants and long underwear, and submerged himself
in the water.

Get some more wood on this fire, the guide said.

Guys rushed to the river and pulled him from the water,

his long arms flailing. He was a big boy—our biggest in the home, maybe three hundred pounds—and drying that much body would take hours.

I turned on the social worker. Better hustle your ass today.

Excuse me?

You know what I'm talking about.

I don't care for your tone. Can you be direct?

Don't be fucking with your straps. Don't fuck with your pack. Don't stop, don't rest, don't do it.

Worry about your own side of the street, she said.

Good Jeff's eyes darkened. What is it with you, he said. Are you mental? Can you not see and hear what's around you? Are you deaf and blind or just stupid?

I am still your social worker, she informed him.

No, he said, you're not. We're through.

Hey, Tommy, Donald said. Guess what day it is! Tomorrow, motherfucker!

Maybe she really did have the soul of a poet and could see into our hearts and knew exactly where we all stood. Maybe she understood my wince at Donald's words or sensed in me that calmness I feel when shit goes down. Maybe she thought my calm signaled something good.

I can't drag the sled, she told me, if I'm going to keep up. I can't carry my pack. I can't carry both. I've tried. I've tried and tried.

Trying's dying, I told her.

Damn it, she said, listen!

What is it you like to say? I asked. Accounta-what-blah-blah-macho-bullshit?

I know all about accountability, she said, but her tone

shifted, and something in this shift allowed me to see her fully as I hadn't seen her this whole time—she'd begun Trip plump, soft, out of shape, but her skin hung loose below her eyes and around her jowls, and her face sagged—she'd lost a lot of weight. I can't do it anymore, she said. I'm tired.

Well, there you go.

Leave her, someone said. Give her a tent and sleeping bag, her skis and whatnot, but let's not be foolish here.

And who was it, I wonder now, who suggested this? Which of our wallflowers had chosen this time to speak up? I don't know. It could very well have been anyone, even the wilderness guide. By now he'd returned from the river and, after slowly untying his boots and setting them by the fire to dry, sat narrow-mouthed, unreadable.

The social worker shook her head. Make you a deal, she said, removing her pack and digging about inside. She pulled her lunch stuff out and laid it by my skis. It's yours, she said, if you take my pack and sled.

I picked up her lunch bag. She had a *lot* of food in that bag. As if she'd been *dieting*. But I didn't think of this then. I thought of the obvious—my hunger and hers for the next week or two.

You won't eat lunch again, I said.

I know.

Donald nodded. The nod said, This here is sufficient; it will do. Take it, man, he said. Fuck her.

Sometimes I wish I had more of a spine and were a hero and didn't think like a criminal—if it isn't me, it'll be someone else; if not this, it'll be much worse. I wish I weren't cold sometimes but kind always and stood up for the meek. In short, I wish I were different, that things were different.

The other boys hungrily eyed the food. Even the guide's stomach rumbled. Meanwhile the woman stared at me, her eyes as wide and vulnerable and unknowing as those of a baby whose face you're about to smother with a goose down pillow.

Mexico

THEY had a way of shifting a suggestion so you believed it was your idea, and a good one at that. From this came a deal—if I agreed to go to Louisiana, I could go to school, play baseball, and get to see my dad one last time. I didn't want to go to Louisiana—no one did—but I needed these other things, same as I needed the illusion of it being voluntary. So I flew down to see him. He was living in an in-law below a friend's house in a small mountain town east of Hemet, California. The town was one of these quirky old hippie places with log cabins and evergreens, friendly diners, four-wheel-drive vehicles. A place where people used chain saws. Signs advertised wood sculptures and ice carving. Life-size replicas of grizzlies and Sasquatch cut from redwood ushered travelers into lodges and the VFW hall. It was February. Snow piled on the side of the road. His car took a while to warm up. He masked the degeneration of his last few years with thick scarves, wool sweaters, an oversize burglar's hat. He did not think it would be long now, a few months is all. This was it. Goodbye.

Catching sight of the two of us in a mirror or storefront window, there was no mistaking our relationship. We are eerily similar. Pictures of us as late teens freak me out. It's not just our eyes and brow, nose and cheeks, the build of our bodies, our long feet and fingers, but the way we hold ourselves, the tilt of our crown, sloped shoulders, slightly stooped, hands in our pockets; how we lean back or forward to talk. And we both have this thing—it's clear—where we will look out at the world and doubt. A haziness obscures our relations. We find ourselves always skirting that rootless cipher of anonymity, known but unknown, in but not of, or of but not in.

We drove through the Coachella Valley and past the Salton Sea, a crystalline body of water in the middle of an arid sink. In the fifties, developers bet on it becoming a famous resort and sold it as the French Riviera for Hollywood—Sinatra played here, Nixon did, too. Retirees came, brought their life savings. But this was a desert, and the Salton Sea had formed by accident, the result of shoddy engineering on a Colorado River dam—there was no way to replenish its freshwater source. It had been stocked with corbina and bass, but the lack of renewable water led to a lack of oxygen which led to the growth of algae which lead to fish breeding which led to more fish which led to less oxygen which led to more death, and so on. Its shores were stacked six feet high with the carcasses of dead fish. Millions more died each day. Former resorts dotting its shores were close to death as well. Towns once zoned for fifty and sixty thousand offered empty gridded reminders of old dreams. Lot after lot sat undeveloped. There were no grocery stores, no restaurants. Abandoned cottages stood on cracked asphalt just past heaps of dead fish. The air thick with stink and death, all that remained were a few people stuck in their investments, lounging in rusted lawn chairs outside faded trailers, waiting for the end.

In Mexico, we got out of the car and walked through a large courtyard beside a cathedral. But his energy had gone. His steps got slower and slower. The wind, he said. It's gotten in my lungs. It's these holes, he told me, in my cheeks. I'll have to sit down.

I helped him to a bench, where he settled his long limbs and closed his eyes.

Would this be it? Was he going to die right here?

Dad? I said.

A slight smile spread across his lips. I'm going to be okay, he said. I'm just—Son? I'm thinking about my mother.

We were in a kind of town square not unlike that place you might imagine in the Johnny Cash song. It was a Sunday morning. Pigeons squawked. Wayward mariachis snoozed on benches.

She was pretty, he said. But not beautiful. She was intelligent, witty, charming, and batshit crazy. She used to get mad at the TV, at things an actor said, and would get up and start kicking the screen or pull it off the wall. She'd get a hammer and break things. She was paranoid, delusional, convinced everyone had it in for her. For most of her adult life, she was institutionalized. Whole decades passed when he didn't hear from her, didn't know where she lived. At some point, he tracked her down via the White Pages, found her in Oxnard, paid her a visit. She'd aged well, he said, was fresh and young-looking. Heavily medicated. He stayed a few nights, and then, just before he left, she laid some truth on him: If you ever visit me again, she told him, you will die.

Or some-such. It's what she meant, anyway, he said. What she implied. You know the thing is, he said, whatever crazy

99

she had, I've got, too. I guess maybe you probably might have some of it as well.

His mouth remained open, his eyes still closed. Was there more? Had he fallen asleep?

Nope. Just caught up in a memory.

Son, he said. Here is the thing—I never knew her. He looked at me. She was always a mystery to me.

I understood him then like I never had before and rarely would again. We were the same. I wanted to hug him. I took his ear in my hand and pulled his head close to my own and held him.

That's nice, he said. It's very nice. Then he tapped my chest. Now let me go, he said. Son. I want to tell you a story, and maybe you've heard this already, I don't know. No one likes to hear the same story twice. Anyway. There're these two bulls up on a hill, looking down on a field of cows. One of the bulls is very young, and the other quite old. The young bull says to the old bull . . . Hold on, son. I have to think. I want to remember how this goes. He closed his eyes and smiled. Yes, he said. The young bull says, Let's run down this hill and fuck one of these cows, but the old bull, he stops him, says, No, why don't we walk down this hill and fuck every last one of them. Again, he tapped my chest. Give me a damn cigarette, he said.

Should you be smoking? I asked.

Are you fucking kidding? Son, I'm dying.

The House

THE House was on West Road, which was the kind of street in a part of a town you'll almost never go. Locals called it Crack Row, and they had reason. Now, of course, our country's drug of choice has changed, as has the neighborhood where it's bought and sold, but back then rock was everywhere, and on West Road you could hear the dopeman, Tree, and his bass long before his lowrider made our block.

Homes here were small, old, manufactured, half-dropped on cinder blocks or bricks; they had unfinished stoops, tinfoil-blocked windows, and plywood exteriors, were missing shingles and doors and doorknobs—I never could tell which were inhabited and which merely used. West Road had so many crack houses that when police came and shut one place down, the next day everyone went next door. Baseheads littered the area. We'd see them pedal their bicycles past the Property, return a few hours later on foot. Like the ranch, it was the middle of nowhere—halfway between Baton Rouge and New Orleans in a truck-stop town of swamp and cypress—and maybe, if you drove past the outlet mall and chemical plants to the levee or into the Maurepas boondocks and Amite, you'd find the beautiful and exquisite—a painted owl, egret, or alligator—yet the House was close in, and all we saw were the broke down, desperate, and washed out. They'd drift by, each day getting skinnier and skinnier until they were only a pile of loose clothes jerking up the road, eyes sunk in their skulls, knuckles, knees, and elbows pushing up through their scabbed skin.

I GOT THERE on a Tuesday during group. Group, they said, is three times a week, mandatory. It's the only thing, Vic said, you got to do, other than not drink.

This was the kind of shit they said.

He snapped a Polaroid, did not search my stuff. Why aren't you searching my stuff? I asked.

Vic, he said, which I'd come to learn he called everyone, and so he, too, was called Vic. Why would we search your stuff? Is there something you shouldn't have? *Vic.* He shook his head. Either you are or aren't. Either you will or won't.

He was a broad-shouldered hulk with Coke-bottle glasses, wearing polyester athletic shorts and a polyester button-down, short-sleeve shirt. He pointed me to the group room.

I was expecting something like the Rockies, except no mountains, snow, or barns—a continuation, maybe, an extension between the two places—but it was completely different. In the boys' home, group offered soft lighting, a warm glow, couches, Kleenex. They encouraged sharing; our feelings were the most important thing. In here, it ran twenty deep. Dudes sat in plastic chairs in a circle, feet tapping. They chewed their nails or the skin on their palms, fidgeted with their hair, mouthed unlit cigarettes. Some of them were old as fuck, like sixty or seventy, and missing fingers or hands, their livers bulging; they had glass eyes, cheap dentures, scars wrapping their heads and faces as if they'd been put together like a puzzle. They wore gym shorts and plastic flip-flops or ill-fitting suits and out-of-fashion ties, all of them with serpentine grins: here is a fresh mouse!

A big biker stalked about, pausing every so often to scribble on a dry-erase board. He had inked-up forearms, black eyes, and was huge, like five-ten, maybe three or four hundred pounds. This was Program. I'd heard about him. Everyone had. He took a look at me. New brother, he said, grimacing. What *is* that shit on your face?

It's a beard, I informed him.

Looks like a pussy to me, he said. Shave it.

Dallas John began rattling his jaw. Something about anxiety or childhood, but it didn't matter. Program cut him off. What the fuck, he asked, are you saying?

I was saying, Dallas John said.

Naw, naw, Program said. I didn't ask so you'd tell me. You need to, he said. If you don't. You're going. Then there's. You'll be strapped. Then. When these mother. And you. You're. Your mom's there, crying. Your dad, well. But your mom.

I couldn't keep up, wasn't sure I wanted to. No matter. There was no slowing down, no welcome packet, no here's what's what. They assigned me a Big Brother, but it was Ray, a psychopath. He brayed in my face, punctuated his noise with catcalls and laughter, then walked away. This was SOP, I'd learn, Standard Operating Procedure: shit always seemed practically on the verge of maybe reaching a point where violence approached. Motherfuckers were loud. They said the word "motherfucker" a lot. Everyone here was either a moth-erfucker, it was known, or a bitch. They said, again and again, All you motherfuckers will die. This was their language, how they conveyed the reality of our disease. Everything nonnego-tiable, no one unique. They were rah, rah, confront, confront, confront: get sober or die, will the real Tom M. please stand up, we've given you the rope, now hang yourself, bitch.

Program just cut on a dime. Hey, he said, before I for-get. Play any fuckaround-fuckaround, kill even a rabbit here, you're going to jail. Play bloody knuckles, jail. Smoke dope, jail. Conspire to rape, jail. This ain't no boys' place, little brother. Playtime is over.

This guy, Dallas John, I guess, was still having some feelings. He leaned forward in his chair, holding his belly. How do you think that makes me feel? he asked.

I don't give a fuck how you feel, Program said.

THEY WARNED ABOUT JUSTIFICATION. What was done was done. Rationalization was the same absurdity. No one cares why. Why is just something to tell people, and what we tell people don't matter. We were all, anyway, just a bunch of liars. Even when we want to tell the truth, we can't, don't know. There seemed no point in questioning this. I mean, who was dumb enough to stand up and say what he really wanted, which 95 percent of the time was to build a bankroll, get up and go, score dope, a girl, a motel room? No one was going to say, Yeah, you know what, I want a razor, a belt, a shoestring, a .38, shotgun, hand grenade, or land mine, a high roof or bridge, a hundred benzos and a glass of water, a shut garage and running car, rope and a rafter, a penknife, whatever. Instead, it's like this: I want sugar. I feel uncomfortable. I miss my mom. All of it smoke and coded. Everything meant something else. Act as if, they told us, or else. And so we did. We said, I want to be here, I want to be sober, I want to live. We knew the people we lied to knew we were lying. That's fine, they said, lie, keep lying, play the rehab game, keep coming back.

In private, we longed for our take on things, that same old why. It was never, in private, what happened. What happened lacks setup, context. You can't con in a vacuum, can't pass the hat without context, there's no Feel sorry for me, no Give me your motherfucking money.

Out in the world, we were men, sons, husbands, and such, but not here. In here, we were drunks, junkies, fuckups, and— bottom line—drunks, junkies, and fuckups will do what they always do, which is stay fucked up and die young. It made no difference, alcohol or drug, pill or marijuana. Same is the same, all of it off-limits now. Sudafed, caffeine pills, NyQuil. If it keeps you awake or puts you to sleep. All of it gone.

They made no distinction between relapse and death. Either case, they said, either way. It's all the same. There's no such thing, they said, as half-pregnant, motherfucker. You can't damn near quit, can you? It's either do or don't.

They preached the disease concept, the notion of craving, how once you scratch an itch, the itch grows paramount, our twenty/twenty tunnel vision, and spoke of its ends in loosely concrete ways: at the edge of town was the White Rose Motel, and brothers who left were said to have gone there, as if this motel were a junkie heaven or hell. Our minds are dangerous, lonely places, and instinctively, same as a kitten paws litter

or a baby grasps tit, we want out, to leave, never mind consequence, never mind wisdom, never mind, never mind. Alone,
lacking outside counsel, we drown, our best right thinking
just a delusion, a kicking and clawing to surface, prolonging
the inevitable. We all promised ourselves things, cut deals: at
the end of ninety days, if nothing is better, I'll tie the noose
myself, and yet within these promises we sought wiggle room,
variance—now, what about a girl, some sweet girl—and in
these fantasies lost track once more of what's known: binge
followed by regret followed by shame followed by another
binge to mask that shame.

Our families were part and parcel of this, and we got
warned off them same as they warned of old using buddies,
or walking certain roads alone late at night, how we find ourselves cruising hard-liquor aisles again and again, or paying
more attention to a beer commercial, or eating too much
sugar, the high of not sleeping, how you hallucinate when
you don't sleep, or feel jittery on your first cigarette, the
adrenaline of bungee jumping—triggers, all. Our illness is
unified, the junkie just the beginning. Call it herpes, you are
the dick sore; in plain-speak: a symptom. Your families don't
know better, they said, but they are just as sick as you. You
must warn them!

They categorized the family tree—addict, hero, mascot, lost
child, scapegoat, enabler—explaining each member's contri-
bution, warned how they'd rotate and shift, bat-shit crazy, all.

You are not alone. Don't have to be. The road to hell is
paved with bricks of goodness, whatever. You are each other's
family now. Be your brother's keeper. You can count on each
other to do right by each other, except when you can't. Stick

with the winners! Secrets keep you sick. Resentments are the number one offenders. Think, don't think!

Our thinking got us here, led us down dark streets, found us outside crack houses at three a.m., knocking on doors, looking to borrow eggs, sugar, and everyday condiments, for this is how our mind works: It's late, I want to bake some cookies, except I'm out of sugar (poor me!). There's sugar in the office, but I don't want to wake the night tech. I can see lights in the crack house across the way. I bet they got sugar in that house, I bet they have eggs!

Stop thinking! No one thinks their way into right behavior. You can't think up a hot dog when you're hungry. It takes action. You must act. The first act is being here. The second is staying.

That's cool, I said, glad y'all found something to help. I'm happy for y'all, truly. Now, no disrespect and all, but I am way, way better than this. Tell me, how long am I supposed to be here again?

WE WERE ALL MALE, age seventeen and up, all loiterers, contributors, delinquents, petty thieves, dropouts, strong-arm men, traffickers, pimps, rip-off artists, pretty-boy hustlers, on loan from correctional facilities, the state and judicial system, referred by thirty- and ninety-day TCs or psych wards, annexed by family, workplace, the military, all of us collected, quarantined, pushed in, fucked.

Guys arrived rough and haggard, nails chewed to the quick, stringy hair greasy or thinned through, wearing threadbare shirts and jeans too long, too loose, or too short, with tattered cuffs or holey asses, and, like me with my goatee, were forced to shave, tuck their shirts in, sew hems, or discard ripped clothing altogether. It didn't matter style, flair, education, or pedigree. Everything became practice in following direction, humility, right action leads to right thinking. Seventeen-year-olds had two options: high school or GED. For anyone not in school, a shit job was mandatory. We flipped burgers, bagged groceries, loaded lumber, cleaned toilets, and dusted shelves, installed carpet and roofing, dug and then built forms, poured concrete, framed and finished houses, changed brake pads and oil, answered phones, hauled furniture from storeroom to showroom and showroom to car, bused tables, washed dishes, mowed lawns, laid sod, shoveled manure, climbed telephone poles, greeted customers at Walmart and retirement homes, or inspected barges on the river. The best jobs of all paid $4.75 an hour.

In total, we were young, old, ragtag, miscollected. If you saw us off Property all at once in a mandatory all-House activity, called a Group Funk, like going to the Circle K or a meeting, on foot and bike, circling each other, clumping up, going lone wolf, straggler, follow the leader, playing grab-ass, fuckaround-fuckaround, pantsing motherfuckers, wedgie-ing bitches, dry-humping fools into lampposts, and wrestling each other to the ground, all of us dissimilar, infinitely specific, terminally unique, and yet fitting together so perfectly hip, slick, and cool, you'd know immediately our situation. My, my, you'd say, look at these halfway motherfuckers.

And yet there was confusion in town, straight mockery: people called it a spin-dry, a group-home, or treatment center. Program didn't buy this talk. You men are in a halfway house, he'd tell us. That means no silver lining, only the inevitable.

We called it the House. Brothers who'd left but remained

in or near town were said to be in *the* area, which was different than *your* area, which referred to a part of the Property you were responsible for cleaning during Checks. Always, as long as we hung around, these words would mean these things. Even after being released, when we rented and owned homes, if we said, Meet me at the House, it meant here.

Of course it was not a house at all but six ordinary two/one apartments lined perpendicular to West Road. It looked like a kind of extended-stay motel where practicing drunks go to die. Dilapidated, with faded shingles, a long and cracked parking lot, and a bent basketball rim in front of Room One, it sat a half mile from Main, and all day and night we watched crackheads twitter down the road. We'd find them wired in our kitchens or rocking in our bathtubs or see them roll from the pines behind our apartments or pull themselves from the gulley, always with that awful look on their face of More. I want more. Give me more. I need more. Our bedroom windows were ground-level, and sometimes when the monsoons came, baseheads pulled our windows open and we'd wake to find ourselves holding them, their bare bellies pressed close for warmth.

A walkway ran the length of these apartments. This was the front porch, an area we were responsible for cleaning. At the end of this walkway, the group room formed an L. Aphorisms and posters covered its walls. A stick figure at a ravine's edge: "When you think you can't, you must." The elusive "Think, don't think." An airbrushed photo of sand, a pair of foot-prints leading to one: God carrying you. The Twelve Steps. The Twelve Traditions. "Come, come to/O, come to believe." A feelings chart with smiley faces—big-eyed, frowning, no mouth, yawn, labeled alarmed, sad, bored, exhausted, and so on—staff referenced after asking how we felt so we'd say something other than fine, which we all knew stood for fucked up, insecure, neurotic, and emotional, which, as they many times explained, isn't a feeling. A dry-erase board gridded with names, admit date, Phase, Hours, Tasks. Drop ceilings, fluorescent lights, a linoleum floor, hard chairs.

The bathroom had crapper, vanity, toilet paper so thin it tore our assholes. A sign-in-sign-out sheet sat on a clipboard on a bookshelf holding coffeemaker, sugar/sugar substitute, nondairy cream, foam cups, A.A. literature. On the bottom shelf were spiral notebooks, our journals. They encouraged us to write in them and read one another's, but we always wrote the same thing: Dear Diary: I am having a good day!

Behind the group room was a four-by-five slab where we sat and talked shit while dudes pumped iron on the rusted weight bench beside it. There was an acre of mowed grass where we played kickball. Beyond it the grass turned scraggly and wild, stretching many acres to a stand of pines beyond which was a field of prairie grass beyond which were more pines beyond which was another field beyond which were more pines, each field sectioned perfectly, cleared but not developed, hopes unrealized of subdivisions and commercial centers, until the pattern stopped and you'd find broke-down cars, rusted swing sets, old basketball courts, a tin-sided liquor store, the projects. Like West Road, these projects were not white or black but a mix, merely poor, bleak, home of the single mother, spinster, drifter, and out-on-bail dad. Finally, there was an industrial park with machine shops fabricating glass, aluminum siding, and steel. Then cow pastures. Trailers. The Waffle House. A few cheap motels. A Shoney's. The Red-Man Truck Stop &

Casino. The intersection of I-10, which led to Los Angeles, and Highway 30, which intersected I-10 again near River Road in Baton Rouge. An outlet mall. Chemical plants. The river.

STAFF CONSISTED OF a few primary counselors, a cook, a couple psychologists, some night techs, and Vic. No one knew Vic's title, not even Program—driver, maybe, mascot. Like the disease itself, he was ubiquitous, foundational. Even when they fired him, he just kept showing up, driving us places, and confronting us until they hired him back. Except the cook, staff were all recovering and claimed they weren't any different from us, only they'd been at it longer—each morning they still had to get on their knees and ask for another day. With them it was always the same: no one is different, you won't make it, your brothers won't, you will all die, one day, even me.

Program, who could be blunt, spoke of five levels: dead, using, dry, clean, sober. Sober offered serenity, a spiritual outlook. It means happy anywhere. It's not a reflection of absence, like clean or dry, but a state of mind. Sober, you can get through anything. Dry was the worst. Dry, you might as well be using. It's all torment, no relief. At least using, there's relief. Even dead, you don't have to feel, he'd say. Dry drunks beat their wives and children. They kill people. Last thing you want to be is dry, he'd say. If you're dry, do the right thing—kill yourself.

Yet for all his rah-rah and bluster, sometimes he'd flip, his black eyes sad, soul bubbling from his chest, and get emotional, ask to lay hands. Palming our arm or shoulder, he'd hover, his three hundred pounds comforting. How are you? he'd ask. How do you feel about thing X? And poof—

Calmness.

None of my answers mattered, all my answers were lies. I was what he said I was. Touching me—I know it sounds gross; it wasn't—holding me, he felt what I felt, for his hand entered my body and attached itself to my heart. I know you, he'd say, I am you. His dark gaze suggested he knew from our behavior how tomorrow would play out yet he offered no condescension, not a smidgen of pity, just calm, flat sadness: this is how it is, nothing you or I can do to stop it. Measured, sincere, supremely confident, he would've made a good politician—he had that kind of self-belief—but his unshakable vision saw only the tragic: all of you will die. He'd randomly select us in group. Tommy, Bill, Ray, Chad, Donny, stand. Here's how many make a year. Tommy, Bill, Ray, sit. Here's who makes two. Look to your left, look to your right. In five years, both those brothers will be dead. I thought, Yeah, okay, these nuts, one out of blah-blah, statistics, what bullshit, in light of my post-Vietnam cynicism, where I see everything as PR, sales, and marketing, let me get this, let me get that, give me your motherfucking money, and so on—

But, man. When he laid hands, it was impossible not to trust, even if I didn't know how. I'd twist it. Like Okay, maybe, for someone else, I get it, you're warning me, but I know you think I'm different. I know it.

He was the first guy I heard say "I'm just as sick as you" who actually seemed to believe it. And he'd tell us. He didn't care. He trusted no one more than us. Not his wife or sponsor. Just us. In this room. And he'd get down to it, offer tales of his old life playing music in Buffalo or Yuma, how he'd walk into roughneck dives dressed as Elvis, his big body rhinestoned and tasseled, a fat show pony, find the biggest and meanest, punch him right in the mouth just to start a conversation. He'd punch the next guy, go right down the bar, like little bunny foo-foo. He'd grab a dude's nuts and twist, kick the back of someone's knees out. He had short, choking arms, powerful hands, and he'd pick men up by their windpipe, watch the lights begin to dim.

Once I found him on the back slab, a far-off look in his eyes, a sliver of wood in his mouth. He asked me if Brother X was using a nicotine patch, and I told him Brother X was quitting smoking. Huh, he said. Have you seen him smoke?

Come to think of it, I had.

He had this way of lifting his eyebrows without lifting them at all.

In subtle glances or brutal honesty, he wanted understanding without prodding. He spoke incessantly of the itch—it covers everything, let it guide you; know, understand, come to love it—and good days and bad, said be wary of both, raged against comfort, feeling comfortable, how stuck we get in ourselves. He'd done and would do horrible things and later was accused of still more horrible shit, allegations that pestered and plagued him to the road once more, but from each infraction he resurfaced roachlike and undead, patiently waiting yet never passive, and though I spent most of these months only half hearing, always with that generational shaking of my hand in front of my nuts—save it, fuck off—I'd come to understand he had too much heart to work a job like that thinking any junkie different. It would've killed him.

* * *

NO ONE COULD SAY HOW LONG I was supposed to be here. It depends, they said. There's no rule book, no set thing. Just fluidity within certain parameters. Common sense governed our behavior, as did consequence. Ignorance was never an excuse. The only hard and fast: don't drink; go to meetings; change your whole life. Everything else was open to interpretation, yet mostly, our interpretations were wrong, and wrong behavior brought consequence, like Stricts, or worse, a form of House-wide Stricts called Flats, where we had to be within three feet of another brother at all times, couldn't watch TV, couldn't leave the Property except for work or during Group Funks, couldn't use the phone, shoot hoops, play cards, lift weights, listen to music, nap, read, etc., etc., etc., and Majors were performed weekly instead of once a month. During Majors, we cleaned obsessively—unplugging appliances, unscrewing their housing, even, pulling them from a wall—using Q-tips, a toothbrush, or our pinkie, detailing hard-to-reach areas; we broke down beds, removed drop-ceiling tiles, pressure-washed everything. Unlike regular cleaning, called Checks, which were monitored by Big Brother Group, staff checked Majors. Any dirt or dust, any gunk or grease, any pine straw, any dead roach or beetle, any anthill, any feather, required us to begin again. If Majors began on Sunday morning, they often didn't end until Monday afternoon. Fuck up on Flats and we got Super Flats, where every brother had to be within three feet of another and Majors were performed every day. You'd see fifteen guys outside a crapper, or one guy shoving a push mower across the backyard while twelve guys trailed behind him.

We got put on Scribes and Ice—no contact, both—and had to stay in the group room corner. The only way off Scribes was to write our way off; we essayed on self-will, sex, powerlessness, resentment, acceptance, etc. Ice meant you were leaving soon, and you just sat there, bags packed, not allowed to talk, read, write, nothing. God help us if we spoke to someone on Ice, for in speaking, we enabled and supported his disease; we, too, would be gone soon. Despite the awfulness of being cut off from our brothers in that corner, we all looked forward to Program tearing ass from the office, eyes black as the Grim Reaper's dick, our sickness evident, hard on the drama, always spitting the same phrase: take two brothers and pack your shit.

The two brothers walked you to your room, ripped your mattress from its bedspring, watched you pack. Is that your shit? they'd ask. Are you sure? It doesn't look like yours. Let me ask—Hey, dick, this your shit? Just making sure. And weird but true, they loved you now more than your mom, kneeling on your floor offering wisdom, strength, hope, or a hug, some advice—The bus station is farther than you think, or A dude I know can take you to New Orleans or Jackson, wherever you need to go—but then, always, once you finished packing, they'd drag your mattress, linens, and pillow to the group room, toss them in the corner, give one last affirmative look before repairing to the front porch, where, dusting their hands, they gathered with the others and their cold drinks and cigarettes and spouted the same old same old: It works if you work it, you can lead a horse to water, Vic, hang around a barbershop long enough, you will get a haircut, any time you point a finger, there's two pointing back at you.

All this, of course, was voluntary up to the point we quit volunteering. Then the police or sheriff or some federal agency showed up and hauled us away.

We got Dress Nice Task, where we had to tuck our shirts into our slacks, couldn't wear jeans or tees, have any tears or frays, or Dress Down Task, where we had to wear jeans and tees. Sloppy guys, on Garbageman Task, dragged their belongings around the Property in a trash bag. Whiners got Crybaby Task and sucked their thumbs. Guys got Sum It Up Task, and Speak Only When Spoken To, everyone had to take the cotton out of their ears and put it in their mouth. Nonconfrontational or overly confrontational brothers got Sheriff Task. Sheriffs wore a gun belt, carried a cap gun and a small notebook, and wrote tickets for shitty behavior such as talking back to staff, swearing, war-storying, anything. Tickets brought fines, a quarter or fifty cents, we deposited in the Confo jar. This was me. I was Sheriff.

We were drama queens, dilettantes, psycho- and socio-paths, head cases, grandiose, delusional, bipolar, suffering from depression, anxiety, ADHD, schizophrenia. We were fatally hip, King Baby all, habitual, practiced, cool. Dudes blew O's when they exhaled. Everyone smoked. Except in group, swearing was prohibited, a ticketable offense—naturally, every goddamn thing was a motherfucking bitch. Failure to make three meetings a week led to Hours. More than three Hours meant Stricts until Saturday Work Detail. Hours and Hours, Hours for everything—too much beard in your goatee, sideburns past your earholes, leaving off a.m. or p.m. when signing out even when clear as day, ashes on the slab, shoes untied in group—no one had zero Hours. We had to belong to home groups, have sponsors, know the steps, be working a step, employed or in school, maintain said job or school, or we got Stricts, no hope of getting out soon.

We needed permission for everything and nothing. No one

said you can only carry X amount cash, but carry more than X amount cash and there'd be a conversation. Paychecks were signed over to staff and doled out as needed for cigarettes, cold drinks, snack foods, what have you. Weekend passes were unusual, family days rare, visitors less than never. If a female came onto the Property, it was by mistake or someone had fucked up and was gone and she'd never find him now, anyway. Sorry about that, sweetie, Program would say, hands dangling over the porch railing, no idea where he is.

Areas rotated daily: living room, kitchen, bathroom, porch. Four brothers lived in each apartment, but on Flats, beds emptied, and empty beds meant multiple areas. Every pubic hair, piece of lint, dead fly in light fixture, gook on stove or crust in microwave, anything in the trash, got you a Mark. Four Marks equaled an Hour. After three Hours, we got Stricts.

There was no lights-out.

At seven a.m., Ranking Brother performed Bed Busts. If asleep (determined by body, not eyes: one foot in bed meant sleeping), we got Hours. Checker came at eight. Our beds had to be made top sheet folded under then over pillow, bed skirt unwrinkled. Nothing allowed on floors, dressers, nightstands, or headboards. A Walkman, a CD player, anything pawnable needed locking up. They opened drawers and closets—were our clothes folded *neatly*? Did shirts *hang* from hangers? What about shoes? Were they orderly? Any infraction, a booger or fingernail clipping, a dust mote, wrinkle, or hair, got a Mark.

Morning Meditation Group. Mantras and affirmations from approved literature. Planning, to-do lists, critiques of, comments on. House Pride, more cleaning. Always cleaning. Each version a different level: Work Detail, Kitchen Clean-up Group, Morning

Checks, Checks, Majors. Each a process of cleaning and then checking. Often by Saturday, there'd be nothing left, except Checker was, by rule, petty, callous, stubborn: the parking lot was cracked, weeds poked through these cracks and needed pulling; pebbles and loose gravel in the potholes needed sweeping, which led to more loosening, leading to more sweeping; pine straw needed bagging, the bags removal; in the gully up and down West, trash thrown from cars needed picking up; the dumpster needed scouring; the front porch—or, if the front porch was clean, a neighbor's front porch—needed whitewashing; here is a toothbrush, detail the parking lines; here is some 409 and a rag, grab the crack dog from the crack house, scrub him.

Apartments, TV, sleep, unapproved literature, basketball, volleyball, cards, and weight lifting were off-limits from eight to three. While some guys went to their shitty jobs, I went to the local high school. The bored, unemployed, or devious signed out on job search. Others sat on the back slab, smoking and trading hard-luck bullshit. Old-timers, usually. They knew what was beyond the Property. They'd go as far as the mail-box, where, hands on hips, they hemmed and hawed about Gerald Ford, quote, waiting for the mailman. What beautiful bullshit. No one got mail. Who'd write? Our sisters? Please. Lord knows what her letter would say. Dear Johnny Raincoat: I'm wondering if you'll ever repay that twenty dollars you stole from my purse. I know it was you! I'd like to buy my son a new action figure. I think of you often. Love, Sandy.

ONE NIGHT, Program pulled Dallas John from a chair and slammed him against the board. This was Thursday night after

Staffing. The wall shook, dry-erase markers fell to the floor. He wrapped his thick hands around Dallas John's throat and began choking him. This is what it's like, he said. It's exactly what it's like.

Guys leaned forward, mouths agape.

Dallas John's eyes were coming unglued. Program's eyes were coming unglued. It seemed their eyes might pop from their faces. Program began a slow, painful wheezing. He released Dallas John and pawed about the board, grabbed at and knocked chairs across the room. His body slackened. He fell over. He was having a heart attack.

Word came he wouldn't make it, and the following days involved much staring at the wild field. Cigarettes still got smoked and stories told, though we lied less now, our bullshit lacked gusto. Guys prepped for the worst, they quit jobs and school, no-showed meetings and therapy. If Program was going to die, we saw no sense in continuing.

Meanwhile, his doctors inserted a catheter into his groin, cut open his chest. They had other ideas, made suggestions. Maybe stay off the Property a few weeks, take it easy, stop wearing jeans and constrictive clothing, eat better, exercise, quit smoking. He'd always warned against self-diagnosis and advocated following professional advice whenever possible, and so he traded his Camels for wooden splinters and chewing gum, bought sandals, triple-XL T-shirts, baggy shorts. And he quit doing group.

Weeds blossomed in the parking lot and dust collected under lampshades, along blinds, and behind washing machines. Hours decreased. Confos dried up. The Sheriff stopped writing tickets. Care and concern reached all-time lows.

Through it all, Program remained watchful, hands clasped over the porch railing or the bed of his truck. A bored smile on his face, he'd paw his mouth and yawn. None of us were fooled. He was like one of those injured wildcats who'll climb into a tree and wait for you to feel safe so that he might pounce down and wrap his jaws around your stupid head. Brothers who normally clamored about him now kept their distance, circling his truck, eyeing him warily.

Come here, he'd say. I just want to talk.

But we stopped just short of ten feet.

This social worker showed up. A normie might've thought she'd investigate the attack on behalf of patient rights, but this was before all that, and we knew better. She had a number of tattoos to suggest she'd been around, and pulled old-school, tough-love shit—I'm talking she'd wait until it rained to kick a brother out. It's a for-the-better-of-the-group, hit-bottom-now, motherfucker, kind of thinking that's mostly out of fashion now.

She put us on Super Flats.

One Step Closer

I went to high school with brothers J-Dog and Mike O. J-Dog was getting out soon. That's what I remember. He gave not fuck one. We'd see him sometimes moonwalking through the cafeteria, hat turned backward, shirt untucked, and shades on. Of course, I'm speaking metaphorically—we weren't allowed to wear sunglasses.

As for Mike, he was never getting out. At least if you asked him. Oh no, he'd say. Not happening. And maybe he knew. Of all the brothers, his story was the most pathetic, or so he'd say: his parents died when he was a baby, leaving him to grandparents who also died, who left him to an uncle who was a fuck who went to jail and left him to the authorities, who left him to an orphanage which found him a foster family who turned him over to another foster family after which came many more facilities until he graduated to youth authority, detention centers, work farms, the correctional cycle, all very so on and so forth, so by the time he arrived at the House, he'd been inside, in one form or another, his entire life.

No one knew where'd he come from this time or when exactly he'd gotten in. He just appeared one night, slumped next to the Coke machine, a small bag of new socks and under-wear at his feet, a pitiful, wanting smile on his face, eyes all Bambi and needful, will you be my friend, please be my friend, can we be friends now?

Like most orphans, he'd developed an instinct for survival that was hard to quantify. He was funny, thoughtful, optimis-tic, everyone's little brother. He'd look at you with his warm Mike O. eyes and suck you right into whatever fantasy he'd only recently dreamed up. He would've made a fine hustler or gigolo, fund-raiser or lobbyist, he had the skill set, he knew what you wanted to hear. If he'd grown old, he might've mar-ried well, lived off an inheritance somewhere ordinary, been country-rich, with riding lawn mower, trampoline, an F350 dually and Winnebago, but he possessed a darkness behind his warmth, and it was clear to all—whatever plagued Mike O. would never be fixed.

He was fifteen years old, by far our youngest, had the dream-boat baby blues, chipped front teeth, thick forearms, wide shoulders, an incredibly thin waist. For all his twisting and pulling, he had true humility: he wanted to be a bodybuilder when he grew up, and pumped iron incessantly. Look at my waist, he'd say. Seriously. Look how thin it is. Tell me, Tommy. Just tell me. Don't be shy. Am I beautiful?

Girls at school adored him. They'd follow us in the cafeteria or jump from behind bushes and trees as we walked to school or wait at that well-worn American divider that is Main (and it was a classic Main, with a water tower, high school football stadium, banks, barbershops, nail salons, downtown athletic club, and auto parts store) until we emerged from the bleakness of West, and they'd slide from their cars with hard candy, chocolates, baked goods, tongue kisses and wet, generous pussies, leggy, beefy-assed, and big-eyed, all. He damn near created an epidemic, what with his sashaying about. Area sales of eye shadow, rouge, lip gloss, and candy-flavored condoms increased tenfold that spring. High heels were out of stock in perpetuity. Even at the outlet mall. Newspapers reported teenage girls wrestling in aisles over hot-pink miniskirts, gouging eyes, pulling hair. They stuffed their bras with toilet paper, socks, and cut-up diapers, cropped their jeans into shorts so impossibly high their ass cheeks wiggled free, slathered their legs with oils and crusted their thighs with cayenne, rosemary, and espresso, quit wearing panties, rolled lollipops over their tongues suggestively, deep-throated drumsticks, bananas, any kind of produce. Nearby grocers noted shortages of squash, cucumbers, zucchini. Ears of glistening sweet corn littered the school parking lot. Regional farmers couldn't keep up, they closed roadside stands, had signs hanging—sold out, gone fishing, retired—and we'd see these farmers potbellied and bloated, waddling from casinos, a hooker under each arm, a cigar dangling from their lips.

Next to Mike, I was invisible. I'd show up first period, set my coffee down, lay my head on the desk, and fall asleep. Drool string from mouth to ear, I walked the hallways half-asleep, the raucousness a sweet lullaby, lockers slapping, girls and girly noises, boys shoving boys into boys and over trash cans and such. I leaned against my locker and dreamed of other places, all better than here.

Dudes slapped my back or desk. Wake up, bitch! You're snoring.

Girls pointed and sneered. Um, you have some crusted-up shit, like, around your mouth?

Yes, I know, I'd tell them. Thanks. Don't worry. It's just drool. Whatever, they'd shriek. Group home!

They'd said I could play baseball. *Said.* No rules against it. Could. Vic brought me to see the coach. We'd hastily scribbled my sophomore year stats on a piece of scratch paper. They weren't great, I admit. I wasn't great. Just eager. But, Vic told the coach, he is from *California.* And tall. Has real quick hands, *I hear.* He offered a few raunchy winks. Maybe he figures it out.

Great, the coach said. We play Tuesday and Friday nights.

Group was Tuesday night. Mandatory.

Oh, no, Vic said. That won't do. Tuesday he's got responsibilities. Is there something we can work out? I mean, he's trying to play college ball, Vic. Missing a year like this—well, it'd be a setback.

Coach leaned back, lifted the ratty scratch paper, and squinted at my stats. He searched about his chest and head and desk before finding a pair of reading glasses. He held the paper to a lamp and turned it several times. Is this here, he asked, a seven or a nine?

Uh, Vic said. Yeah. I believe it's a four, Coach.

Yah-huh, Coach said. I see. Well. He can work out with us. If he wants. But I can't have no part-timers. Can't have a guy showing up only sometimes. Wouldn't be fair to my guys. He pushed back from his desk. There's always legion ball in the summer.

I THOUGHT PEOPLE felt sorry for me. And maybe they did. Teachers let me sleep. When their pacing or scratching the chalkboard woke me, they'd offer an apologetic glance and

I'd get up without a word, stumble to the bathroom, choke down cigarettes until I felt jumpy and vague.

No one said dick.

After school, I worked out with the team: batting practice, bullpens, shagging flies. I was a curiosity, I guess. Guys showed interest. They'd see me in the bathroom and pause. What's it like? they'd ask. And I'd lie: Not bad. After practice, they gave me rides, offering quiet sideways glances at me as we passed one crackhead or another, or back on Property, car idling, eyes downcast, not wanting to see the line of old-timers leaned against the porch railing with their coffee and cigarettes and phlegm, another question in their throat, so full with it they choked.

Eventually, Coach pulled me aside. Listen, he said. I'm a man of my word. You can still work out with us, but you got to do it on that other field. He pointed toward a weedy field. It was empty. Too many mouths to feed, he said.

I thought I could get away with anything. I skipped whole periods, smoking. What can you say? I'd ask. How you fixing to punish me? Nothing could be worse than this. People knew me as that guy pacing and fretting about the john, or brooding, a foot on the sink, a half dozen butts crushed into the windowsill. What are you doing? guys on the team asked. What the hell you thinking? You can't touch the already touched, I said. Or Mike joined me. These were the best days. We'd share unrealistics, pretend life was something else, as if, after school, I wouldn't be on the bastard field and tonight we'd be normal, in six weeks we'd take spring break in Texas or Florida, bang pussy, maybe even have ordinary high school relationships, look forward to prom, dread meeting Daddy, whatever kids do.

I kept going to that far field. There was so little for me—just a batting tee and tire. Sometimes a guy who'd fucked up got sent over in penance, and we'd throw long toss or soft toss.

Oh, don't worry about me, I'd tell them. I'll be balling come motherfucking summer. Hey, watch this. Watch my hands. They're like lightning. Want to play patty-cake, how about down-down baby? Do you like ninja slap?

I kept going. Afternoons all sprint, walk, sprint, walk. Jogging. Pick up a ball, set it on a tee, pick up the ball, set it on the tee, step-hit-hands. I stretched a lot. Every muscle. Run poles. Stretch again. Where else would I go? At home, they were doing Standing Honesty Groups that lasted four hours because some guy couldn't cop to eating fifteen Pop-Tarts. They were playing spades, maybe smoking on the back slab, sweating balls and telling stories, or doing dyads, or sitting outside Program's office while Program called their mom, or waiting for Vic to take them to Baton Rouge to the regional headquarters of McDonald's for orientation and uniform.

Across the street from the field was the library, and one day, in a clump of trees on its south side, I saw girls. A lot of them. All lined up, like outside a concert hall. They were all reaching into their halter tops or skirts and removing their panties and bras, balling them up, hurling them through the air. I sprinted to right center to get closer.

Mike O. was propped against an elm, a blade of grass in his teeth, twirling, I believe, an eye patch, while this long line of beauties waited patiently to serenade him.

They told us junkies take junkies down, that we actively seek witness, someone to hold our hand, tell us it's okay, and when someone wants to relapse, he'll find someone else to fall, too. This wasn't hard and fast, they admitted, and true to form, we saw plenty disappear when no one was looking, only to resurface months later cocaine-thin in a checkout line at Piggly Wiggly, buying Brillo pads and baking soda, the tools of the crackhead's trade. And while being in that grass was off-limits for Mike O., even by witnessing, I was complicit. They called this a Negative Contract, and it was the biggest no-no in the House. Bigger even than using, NCs got us Flats or booted. It didn't matter how we got one. If someone sought us out, if they said, Hey, Tommy, I fucked a girl in the bathroom at Shoney's last night, I don't know her name, didn't wear a condom, she was drunk, I met her in the video poker room at the Redman truck stop, I bought her the booze, I'm not even sure she's eighteen, and you know what, I liked it, we were required to call group. In group, we'd say, I called this group out of concern for Brother X, and we'd rat that fucker out to brothers and staff. If we didn't, if we just said, Hey, you know, that's cool, don't worry, it don't mean nothing but a roll in the hay, or It happens, pray about it, or any of the things we say when someone tells us things, we entered into a covenant with that person, a Negative Contract, a secret, and as the saying went—what they told us—secrets keep you sick.

But Mike O. just had this thing about him. He struck every one of my codependent nerves. And he knew it. He waved kind of playfully.

I tipped my cap, jogged to home plate, sprinted back to center. By now he'd stood up and taken one of the girls by the hand and was leading her into the woods. I sprinted to home, trotted to left, sprinted to right center, beelined for second, and sprinted back to right center, but he'd disappeared.

*   *   *

SCHOOL SUSPENDED ME for assorted minor offenses. The first time in-house. Sit in the cafeteria a few days, no biggie. I leaned back, flipped pencils at the ceiling, clodhoppers next to my smokes and lighter on the table, two middle fingers or crotch-grabbing if you looked at me. Didn't tell Program. Or the brothers. Only Mike. And we had contracts now.

I didn't change.

The next time I got suspended, school called Vic, said, Come pick his ass up. Vic came, told me what he always did: Baseball players don't smoke. I told him I knew that already. He said, Program's not going to like this. Same for the brothers back at the House: Motherfucker, are you crazy?

I went to see my Big Brother, Ray, that psychopath. A criminal archetype who possessed the kind of bad that will never be good and knew it, he used to strut about with this psychotic grin that said, I know what you're thinking, I thought it already, have my response, your response to my response, and my response to that, too. He'd done time for the usual possession, intent, burglary, B&E, aiding, abetting, and contributing, placing body fluid on an officer of the law, etc., but also the more complicated and sinister assault, robbery, hostage taking. He faced a great number of years—the state minimum in Oklahoma, where he came from—for kidnapping if he didn't complete the House, but he was beyond hip, slick, and cool and didn't care. Even our hardest old-timers, real criminals who'd gone federal, admired him. He spent a long time in the House, much of it Ranking Brother, worked his way up Big Brother Group from Rec BBG to Kitchen BBG to Checker BBG to Chief BBG, and had, it seemed, reached an understanding with Program where he could do his own thing, more or less, just don't use, don't bring any of my guys down with you. Staff let him buy a car. Fucking with us was a familiar joke to them, like they'd make a gambling junkie get a job emptying ashtrays on a riverboat, or allow someone like Ray use of a car. We've given you plenty of rope, they'd laugh, to shove up your own asshole.

Late one night, my first week in the House, I'd watched Ray saunter back on Property well after curfew, a bootable offense, but he didn't even hesitate, just strutted up to me. What the fuck, he asked, are you looking at? He wagged his finger playfully. Don't ask, he said, what you can't handle knowing.

I found him now on the back slab with his posse. He had a stick in his hand and was beating it against the concrete. What the fuck do you want?

When I told him, he just laughed. Fool, he said. You think they'll kick you out, but they won't.

That night in group, Program stalked brother to brother, taking each one in, eyes twinkling, opening his mouth to speak, and then no, he'd save it or not yet or not worth his time or there's too much of you to get into. For now, anyway.

I realized he was still standing in front of me. What's up? I said.

What's up? He looked around to see if I was talking to someone else. *What's up?*

I don't know, am I stupid or what? I leaned forward. Yeah, I said. *What's up?*

Oh, man. Program shook his head. Little brother, I don't get you. But you need to get me, he said. If you don't, I'll take away baseball. Then I'ma come down to that school, pull your ass right out, make you get your GED. I'll have you flipping fucking burgers, making motherfucking milk shakes.

I'll tell you how life in the House goes: you become fast friends, and because of this you'll get in a car with your new fast friend and go somewhere, but that place won't be the place you thought you were going. I believe Ray signed us out to a meeting. It was Friday night. He had his usual crew. Rick K., Atlanta John, Chad H.: the cool guys, basically, all of them in their jeans and wifebeaters, eyes glazed, not giving fuck all. We drove to Baton Rouge. He let them off on Chimes. This is all bars, head shops, tattoo parlors, typical college scene. No idea what they were doing, though I could guess. Next he drove to Alex Box, LSU's baseball stadium. Under lights, the field glowed, grass so shiny it seemed wet, foul lines stark white, purple and gold flags, deep crimson on the horizon west of the levee beyond the right-field wall. It was beautiful.

He bought me a ticket, nachos, a dog and cold drink, Cracker Jacks. He leaned back and watched the game. While he watched, I watched him. He didn't like this, or pretended not to. He shoved my shoulder. C'mon.

I couldn't help it. The dude scared me. It wasn't physicality but how cool he was. Cool. Not *GQ* but cool. Real cool. Nothing fazed him.

Listen, he said. You got to stop fucking up at school. How you fixing to play ball if you're not in school anymore? He'll take baseball from you, just like he said. Isn't this your thing? Isn't it what you love? It's what you're going to do, right?

I hope so.

The fuck you mean, *I hope so?* His jaw tensed. I got offered a scholarship to play football. Did you know that?

I can't picture you in school.

How's that? he asked.

I'm just saying.

Just saying. Shit, if you think I'm dumb, say it, he said. I know what goes on at school.

Nothing goes on there.

Pfft. After school.

I go to practice.

I've driven by there.

And?

Wait. He squinted at me in disgust. Are you? A *virgin?* He could barely say it. You are, aren't you?

I wanted to sound tough. Hell, yes, I said. I'm saving myself.

Are you kidding? He searched the stands, as if wanting to escape. Fuck you, nancy, he said. I'm mad, actually pissed. At *school?* He leaned forward and spit. How are you a virgin at school?

It's not like I'm trying to be.

Trying's dying, fool. I mean, look. It's a fairly simple process. You stick your little dick in their pussy. It's easy. All you got to do is look right in their eyes and smile. Then their pussies water.

Pussies don't water, I said, though honestly, I wasn't sure.

Whatever, virgin. What's the furthest you been, anyway?

Blow job, I said, which was true, though she'd been a hooker.

Huh. How much you pay?

Twenty-five bucks, I admitted.

He whistled. Not bad. And what his name?

Program.

You're lucky he didn't kill you. Ray shifted his weight, pulled a tin of Kodiak from his pocket, and began whipping his finger against it. I'm looking at a long time, he said. Do you know what I'm saying?

I knew what he was saying. Yeah, I said. Contracts.

I JOGGED THE OUTFIELD ON MONDAY, scanning the trees, but Mike wasn't in them. That's what happened. Where was he? I wondered. Who was he with? I stopped running. Running made no sense. I walked back to the dugout, untied and removed my cleats, peeled off my socks, pants, cup, and jock, slid on a pair of shorts. I placed a ball inside my glove, put everything in my bag.

Coach was on the mound, addressing the subtleties of holding a runner on first. Shoulders hunched and cap pulled low, he looked to first, then into the catcher's mitt. Quick glance at first. Long stare toward home. Maybe he heard the dugout gate or felt it. Just before I turned to the library, he stepped off the bump.

He was holding a ball in his right hand in a way I'd held a ball all my life. It's the way you hold it before throwing it in your glove and popping the leather, which is how you break in a glove and something you might do a hundred times on any given day, so much that, even alone in center field, you will pound your fist into your glove from habit, and I expected him to do this now as he watched me pull the gate shut and take sight of him and my would-be teammates huddled on the mound—C'mon, I thought, pound that leather, pop it, be normal—but Coach just looked at me, and in his eyes I saw my own history with this sport, the love I'd felt when I first picked up a bat, how ever since, it'd been all I wanted to do, and his look seemed to say, I get it, circumstances change, sometimes there's nothing to do but accept it. He nodded. And I walked away.

Some of the Brothers

RANDY G. was forty-three, had a haircut by Flowbee, a hunched back, shoulder fat, a child's thin legs. Before the House, he'd lived with his mother in a postwar prefab in Cleveland, Ohio, where he worked at an art-supply store, was a huffer of glue, Magic Markers, a garbage-can junkie. I'd like to say his story ends well, but he slammed Dilaudid in the group-room john and Program told him, Take two brothers and pack your shit. Randy G. was gone.

Andy C., seventeen, had a baby face, baby-blue eyes, head razored to the scalp. He stood five foot one, weighed a hundred pounds. In another life, he might've been a featherweight fighter, coxswain, or jockey, but in this life, he was a heroin junkie and gutter punk, a dumpster diver and panhandler. He wore a black bomber jacket, black cargo pants, and twenty-eyed Docs. I don't know what happened to Andy. He left one day. Disappeared. Gone forever.

Jack Rehab, twenty-four, had been a logger until he freebased cocaine. Gleeful, exuberant, he quit cutting and climbing, pawned his chain saw and ax. He was in love and, like any romantic fool will do, followed his heart. Some guys he knew sold rock from their home. They were slobs, their house a mess. He cut them a deal—I'll clean your home for whatever. While he scrubbed, they threw stones—Here, bitch, scrub, bitch, clunk.

Rehab had stringy hair and rotting silvery teeth, wore shoes and clothes gone out of fashion many years ago, but had come to revelation and would do whatever it took. He had the lingo down, could recite the Twelve Steps one to twelve and twelve to one, knew verbatim the first five chapters of the Big Book and most of the stories. God-fearing, spiritual, grateful, and willing, he would go to any length.

Andy P., nineteen, Virginia, had been full of promise at one age. I can't remember his drug of choice. Coke? Pot? I don't know. I have no memory of him breaking Stricts, stealing Confo money, or wiping his own Hours off the board. He was a wallflower. No idea what became of him. Best guess he's using now, dead, or married and living a bland life with offspring full of promise who'll grow up to be junkies who push their mom down the stairwell.

Three Dog came from Luland, Metairie, or Kenner, wherever he felt like that day. His mother lived in Kenner, his aunt in Luland, his grandfather in Metairie. His dad was dead. He'd split time between the three places, and you could fuck yourself if you didn't get why he claimed all three. They were all the same anyway, bedroom communities outside NOLA. His dad had been a surgeon and his grandfather, too, or politicians—a real prominent family—and he was supposed to be a surgeon as well, only he'd made the same crucial discovery as Jack Rehab. Here's a fourteen-word story: rock cocaine will make your ass feel real, real good, for a little while. Now Three Dog looked forward to five years if he didn't finish the program. No one cared. We made a pool when he got in, gave him three days, a week, tops.

Like quite a few, Jon B., nineteen, got in claiming no DOC, just recreational use. He was, he said, more or less a good guy. Not one clue, he insisted, why I'm here. But as with Rehab and Three Dog, you could see it in his teeth: dinned and silvery, from a distance you might think he'd been drinking a heavy red, but once you got closer, if you listened to the spaces instead of the words in his stories, you'd say, Nope, that's not cabernet on this boy's teeth, this fool's been smoking rock cocaine.

There is also the story of the old man who, like Mike O., had true humility—a fundamental understanding of who he was, who he wanted to be, and an earnest desire to get there. We called him Sweet Daddy. Fifty-three, a crackhead from Gary, Indiana, he showed up speaking nonstop of a woman back home. She was his impetus for sobriety, his one true thing. Later, he would speak of other matters, and later still, he grew to speak of everything, be it the relative merits of Formula 409, the streaking patterns left on windows by paper towels versus newspaper, or his feelings about sobriety. We would have called him Captain Planet, I suppose, except he didn't seem to give a fuck about rules or what he had to clean, what he could or couldn't read, when he could sleep, watch TV, nothing. Checks didn't bother him. Majors was just another day. Three meetings—pfft, he'd make five. He lived for Kitchen Crew; Group Funks were better than flying solo. His journal and Big Book always at hand.

Dude blew my young mind.

Habitual and steady, he freely named himself—he had alcoholism, the disease, was a vampire, would suck the life right out

of you. Now, he was on a mission back to his woman, and he'd
go to war, the moon, Mars, or Venus, a distant ring of Jupiter
if he had to. He described her smooth skin, the intricacies of
her breath and heartbeat, her sense of humor, the way she
laughed at herself or bit her lip, how she hummed, her whole
body vibrating when he'd nose her ear. He had the feel of a man
who'd thought so long about a thing that it had become him.

I began to wonder if she was even alive.

Timmy D., a common drunk, was so old and brittle we had
to keep him out of the wind. Somewhere between forty-five
and seventy and six foot four, weighing 115 pounds, he hailed
from Gulf Shores, Alabama, where he'd been an offshore pipe
fitter on rigs. You don't have to be an OSHA rep to know
booze and a welding arc don't mix. The fingers on his right
hand were fused to his wrist. He had to use a forearm to ignite
a Zippo, but ignite that fucker he did.

I didn't think I belonged: I was very young. Only Mike O.
was younger.

Chad H., twenty, had glazed eyes, permanently dilated
pupils. They were a consequence, same as wretched kidneys
or Timmy D.'s hand, and Program said they'd stay that way—a
while—but Chad was all whatever. He dressed grungy, granola,
urban hippie. DOC: heroin. When he spoke, his words mir-
rored his pupils—slow, elongated, blurred. He rarely made
meetings, worked the steps only to satisfy Phase, and generally
did not care. In a perfect world, he would've made a fine wallflower like Andy P., but Ray liked him, and that meant trouble.

Lionel, seventy-five, a common drunk like Timmy D., was
the oldest brother I saw. A dinosaur, really, he'd enter group
with his arms crossed already, sit down, lean back, yawn, and

cross his ankles. He spoke dubiously in grunts and fuck-yous and privately doubted he was an alcoholic—if such a thing even exists, and it doesn't!—but as much as he wasn't, he was a hell of a lot closer to one than any of us. He'd spilled more liquor than we'd drunk, smelled more than we'd seen, and so on. Of course he would die alone, leaving behind children with holes in their chests and mixed feelings, wreath already wilted.

Atlanta John, a has-been college baseball star, used to play catch with me in the grass behind the group room. He had a good arm, was tall, handsome in a surfer way, with iced-up highlighted hair, a perfect nose, strong chin. He was enterprising. He carried a backpack filled with a variety of cigarettes he sold on Property for a marginal profit. This was a no-no but also convenient, and no one was ratting him out. He made a few bucks. So what. It saved us a trip. But things got bleak for Atlanta John, or they got good, and he bought a couple twelvers of Coors Light and visited a No Contact brother named B (nineteen, crystal meth, HIV-positive) who lived in a trailer across Main. They drank and shot crank and fucked each other until they died.

Steve G., a musician, disappeared quietly back into the never-never of wherever he'd come from.

Chad C., coke, died of a heart attack at twenty-one.

None of us had been boys who raised our hands in class. We'd sat in back, stared out the window, etched initials into our desks, looked off one another's papers, popped gum, yawned, snapped what's-her-face's bra, spat wads of phlegm into palms we wiped on our jeans or the back of your shirt. In the bathroom, we sniffed glue or choked each other out until we felt light-headed and good. At recess, we fought or hooped or repaired to the woods to smoke cigarettes and weed and light pine straw on fire.

In total, we were men who began early and could not cope, kicked out of here and there, who'd been molested by or molested our brothers, sisters, fathers, mothers, uncles, aunts, cousins, babysitters, coaches, neighbors, priests, teachers, coworkers, dealers. We all faced jail or the road, but we were all tough, stubborn, bulletproof.

Jack Rehab left on a bicycle, pedaled right off the Property and down West Road toward the highway, a suitcase dangling from each handlebar. We all stood at the Property's edge, smoking, placing bets, watching him stomp pedals, his body jerking one way and then the next, trying to balance the unequal weight of his luggage. It was pathetic, triumphant, pathetic.

In March, I lived in the back bedroom of Room Four, window, a bunk bed. Lionel the alcoholic slept wall, and because the House was crowded that spring, Andy C. slept below me. In the front bedroom were Jack Rehab and Sweet Daddy.

Sweet Daddy spoke of ordinary sunshine through glass, winter in Gary, dirty snow piled up along the sidewalk, rusted-out cars, the meat loaf his woman cooked, her mashed potatoes and gravy. We never got a name. It was just his *woman,* his *girl,* my *lady,* their link so tight that after all the years and transgressions, a name didn't matter. This is how love is, he seemed to say, pay attention, young bucks. His talks took place outside the group room near the Coke machine, positioned to watch the road or hear the phone ring. He spoke slowly, measured. He rolled the tip of a Newport between his thumb and index finger. Some tobacco came loose, fell to the ground at his feet. Standing up was a procedure. He'd palm his thighs and lean forward, and brothers would ease toward him in case he didn't make it.

He'd done such fucked shit that the most fucked thing he could have done was just a blip, an afterthought, he only considered in relation to his movements. And all his movements circled back to her. He spoke of everything about her, called her pussy a pie. This was what it came back to—that whole show. Everything else a cherry on top, the icing, crumbs on your macaroni and cheese, and yet he didn't speak about their lovemaking in some dirty, lowbrow way, but instead as beautiful, necessary.

How long, he asked, are we supposed to be here?

No one could answer. No one knew. There was no answer. We were here, it was understood, until we weren't.

We'd all seen, heard, or known of someone who'd walked in four or five months. Psycho Ray, on the other hand, was approaching a year.

Like Sweet Daddy, guys spoke longingly of the outs, places they'd been or were going, movies currently showing, movies we'd miss. Mike O. talked about his foster homes, how no one cared. He described his foster parents, by and large check collectors, none of them terrible people; it wasn't like that. I talked about the commune where my mom took us when we were kids. And my dad. That's where I'd go, I told Mike. If I left. Either place. You should come, too, I told him. I've called them. They got a farm. If we work on it, we can live rent-free. Timmy D. talked about his wife—he missed her—and Ray talked about his mom. Nob remembered the Carolina shore, and Captain Ron dreamed of joining the air force. Hair-pie, who was different, who wore loafers and pleated slacks, whose

141

drug of choice was not a drug at all but spending money, who came from an old family that could trace its heritage, land rights, and chattel to the days of European aristocracy, who used to sit behind the group room—quiet and alone and meditating—who never got a sponsor, nor tried to make Phase, who was so grandiose he was proud of his grandiosity, who said his Verbal of "Hello, my name is Hair-pie, and I think I'm better than you" with such gusto and verve staff changed it to "Hello, my name is Hair-pie, and three things I admire in you are," spoke of his now deceased father, his two younger siblings, the family he'd have to steward, the pressure he felt. G-Dub, who was bald up top and had a mullet in back, talked about the guns he owned. E-Dog spoke of crystallized sunsets over the New Mexico mountains, how the sky bled deep inky blues and heavy grays when a storm approached. Guys talked about jam bands—Phish, the Dead, Widespread—and touring. They talked about nitrous tanks and the quick goodbye of darkness. They talked pinpricks, constipation, the itch, air bubbles in syringes, and argued could you or could you not die from air bubbles. They talked about going up, coming down, dicks cocaine-limp. They talked about the taste of gun oil, how a rope feels around your neck. They talked meds, pharmaceuticals, various shrinks and shrink methodology. And yet for all the bragging, minimizing, and half-truths, we rarely spoke about wanting to die. Kill yourself in the House, the thinking went, and your ass was in trouble. Even mentioning it brought consequence. We called "I want to kill myself" the magic words. Say them and get shipped. Older dudes, veterans of treatment centers, institutionalized all, spoke around it. They had "dark thoughts" or "felt blue." But one night in group this sad sack said he wanted to kill himself. Fretting, worried, he wrung his hands and tore at his hair. I wondered what the others thought. They looked around. No one was dumb enough to say this aloud.

Well, Program finally said. Life ain't for everyone.

And though we started pools, gave new brothers Three Dog or any of the Andys a couple of days or a week, tops, from the beginning, no one questioned Sweet Daddy. I've told you how rules didn't bother him. He had willingness. He wanted. He was so meticulous in his area that from nine p.m. on, you'd never see him without 409 and rag in hand. He spoke lovingly of our cook, could never get enough red beans and rice and buttered rolls, and though Sweet Daddy's availability wasn't unusual, the tenacity of his openness alarmed us. He needed no prodding to share his experience, strength, and hope; his words didn't feel like bullshit, weren't false, not a game or smoke. I couldn't figure it out—none of us could. Was it his age? The weariness of surviving so long? Maybe he just wore out.

His humility disarmed even our most fervent dickbags. To see him walk the way he walked, all slow, ass out, back curved in pain, how long it took him to reach down and wipe a toilet's rim or pull weeds from the cracked parking lot, or get on his arthritic, crackling knees and run a wet finger along the edge of the crown molding, was to believe.

All he wanted, he explained, was to get right so he could get back to Slidell and see her one more time.

Slidell? a guy asked, astonished. Slidell is in Louisiana, of course, and Gary in Indiana, and this brother, a real jackass, I suppose, leaped from his chair. Is that where you're from?

No, Sweet Daddy said. I am not.

143

But that's where your woman is, I prompted him, but Sweet Daddy did not respond. He just sat there, rolling his cigarette back and forth in his fingers, his memories and secrets so beautiful and reckless and troubling that he had no space left, no capacity, to answer a question like that.

He'd arrived on the scene late one Friday night with a man named Darryl, who was forty and a crackhead, in a long white passenger van coming from some other place. They got out and set their bags by the office and sauntered over to Room Four, where some of the guys were Group Funking war stories and whatnot. We were on Super Flats.

They were both so damn old. Retirement home is on Main, one of the brothers explained.

Sweet Daddy smiled. Like I said: he gave not fuck one.

Darryl, on the other hand, hunched over and wrinkled his nose at the Property. His eyes fell on our dilapidated basketball hoop, and he scowled contemptuously. He took in the group room, dumpster, Coke machine, and apartments. His face grew sad, full of regret.

Guys were blowing O-rings, waving at gnats and mosquitoes. I watched one moth after another slow its wings, land on the lantern above, buzz crisply, and die. One more thing to clean.

Then a noise like gunplay erupted on West, and a 1965 Lincoln Continental coasted onto the Property. This was the height of the hooptie era, and in Los Angeles, Dr. Dre and Snoop Dogg were probably bumping down Sunset in a hybridized version of this exact model, but pop culture comes slowly to southeastern Louisiana, and this Continental hadn't been restored, lifted or lowered, or outfitted with any twenty-four-inch spinners. Utilitarian rather than flashy, an old man's ride, a once-things-were-good-but-all-good-things-end kind of car, it turned in to a parking space and idled just long enough for a suicide door to pop open and for Timmy D. to tumble out, followed by a suitcase. He staggered in the back-draft of his disappearing ride as the Continental reversed off the Property and into the night. I'm already on record about Timmy D., how frail he seemed, how hesitant in the wind. He staggered forward as if weighed down by chains.

Don't get your hopes up, Darryl told him right off. It's not what I expected. Again, he scanned the Property, as if looking for something more.

I admit the place wasn't pretty. It looked like a place where you might find drugs or a dead hooker, not sobriety.

They said over the phone my wife can't visit, Timmy D. told Darryl, and then looked at us. Is this true?

Guys shrugged. We didn't know. There were different rules for everyone. Probably. Then someone mentioned an awful truth. Was that your wife, this dick asked, who dropped you off?

No, Timmy D. said. That was not my wife. His tone straightforward, intelligent, he understood the implication.

Darryl wanted to know what we did, like for recreation and so forth.

Now we wrinkled our noses. Someone laughed. Clean. Therapy. Group. Our one-word answers a collective accept it or die, get bent, fuck off. Clean. Clean again. Clean and clean. Clean some more.

What all, he asked, could y'all possibly clean?

Everything!

Yup. He turned to Sweet Daddy. I was expecting something else.

A Newport appeared in Sweet Daddy's hand, and he tapped its butt against his thumbnail. His grin cool as cool is, he'd been around before and knew what we meant. Leave, if you want, we don't care.

Y'all be kind. Ray smirked. Sometimes we go to the store.

The store?

Sure. Cigs n' Suds. Circle K. You know.

They told me there was a pool, Darryl said.

It was an old, cruel joke and Ray mentioned this now, laughing.

And a gym?

There's a weight bench behind the group room.

Y'all are all so young, Darryl said, which was what people often said of us in a disparaging way, though we could tell he didn't mean it like this. He was just scared.

Timmy D. stretched and yawned. Well, he said. I guess I'll turn in. I've had quite a long day. So if one of y'all will show me to my room—

Can't, we said.

Why not?

Flats, Ray said, grabbing Mike O. by the neck and rough-housing him about. Someone suggested Group Funking an ass-whooping, and a few of us pushed Ray over the railing into the mud, where we wrestled at him until he grew tired of it all, turned us on our bellies, and dry-humped us triumphantly into the ground.

Fuck this, Darryl said, and began walking toward the road.

Where you going? Sweet Daddy asked.

Darryl waved his hand. I'm leaving.

Man. Sweet Daddy pointed at the office. Don't you want your bag?

Darryl eyed his suitcase, still upright by the office door. No, he said, considering it. I don't think I do. He walked into the middle of the road, looked east toward downtown and then west toward the familiar crack houses, where men circled strawberries slinging snatch a ten-rock a pop, and twittered along the gullies or emerged zombie-like from the woods, and babies cried on front porches, and preteens took up sticks and shards of plywood and beat each other in gravel drives.

Dud, from Plano, heroin, who always wore jeans, used to get so angry his pimples turned white. He did terrible things in the House, bullying things, stuff so mean I felt bad for him—what kind of childhood must a man have to turn out this way? Many years later, in fact, he came after me one night with a tire iron, but despite his temper, when we were in the House, when I'd cry, he'd hold me in his arms. Years passed in the usual way. Eventually, Dud stuck a .32 in his mouth and swallowed a bullet.

Ditto Tim S., thirty, an alcoholic.

We didn't consider ourselves anything other than trapped. Not by the Property or circumstance but deluge of fact. Still, if what they said was true, we were relatively safe here, as long as we followed rules. A stillness emerged, patterns, routines. And yet in this stillness, we longed for the sudden and grotesque. Guys bounced basketballs off one another's faces, threw plates of food at each other, and wrestled about like dogs, but if we actually laid violent hands on one another, we got arrested, jailed, prosecuted.

A Johnny R., who was local, showed up. Thirty, a crackhead, he possessed a self-will run so riot he wouldn't clean his area, do dyads, or take meds. He skipped one-on-ones and group.

He didn't like being here, hated the counselors, the food and bedding, all of us brothers. The feeling was mutual. He had sun-reddened skin, a widow's peak, always scowled. Rehab loved confronting him, always face-to-face, always with his Say, bra, that ain't how we do it. Eventually, red-assed Johnny got violent with Rehab in the mud between the group room and the office, and we all jumped the railing and piled Johnny, scrummed him, tugged his ears, pushed his eyeballs into his brain. The police found him half-naked, covered in blood and spit, and yet he'd started it, so they arrested him. Good. Johnny was gone, we thought, but he was from here, and we saw him many times at meetings after that, picking up one desire chip after another as if trying to fill an entire drawer with them.

Joe Morning Wood was a twenty-two-year-old heroin junkie who'd many times OD'd and died. He had long eyelashes, freckles, what people might call a "button" nose. He seemed quiet at first, shy: all the times he'd OD'd and died, he'd been brought back, but then one day he sat down in a shooting parlor next to a teenage girl who'd never shot dope, and so Wood cooked some dope, tapped her vein, stuck the needle, hit the plunger, and this girl, the virgin, OD'd and died. She did not get brought back.

Nob was from North Carolina and a speedball junkie.

Hymen, Florida, cocaine.

A lot of guys came in with a change of shoes, some socks and underwear, a few pairs of jeans, a Walkman, some ratty tees. Ray, on the other hand, showed up with only the clothes and shitkickers he wore, a flannel jacket folded over his shoulder, and a copy of the Big Book. Vic, Vic said, don't you got a bag or something, but Ray did not.

Scott, thirty-four, Houston, cocaine, had been part of some unspeakable thing. No one knew what, exactly. I recall bits and pieces and sadness. Another hard-core Joe Sobriety type, Scott also carried 409 and a cleaning rag everywhere. He worked long hours cooking in a hotel and never stopped moving from job to Kitchen BBG to House chores, no complaints. It always seemed to be this way with unspeakable pasts.

Years later, I was sitting in the office with Vic when a social worker came in holding an envelope. I have no idea, she said, who this motherfucker is talking about. She handed me the letter. Any clue?

The letter was from Scott's father. It thanked everyone. It was a death notice, I think. Scott had disappeared. He was using again when he did. This was sufficient.

Corey, seventeen, crack, relapsed with Pete D. (forty, an appliance or car salesman, claimed it didn't matter—he could sell anything) on rock a few doors down from the Property.

This was SOP. We had a pay phone outside the group room, and Tree's runners used to leave ten-rocks in the coin-return slot. We'd come home and find baseheads on our couches or shivering and fetal in our bathtubs. Strawberries pranced about our parking lot, wearing T-shirts and nothing else, and they'd spin on their bare feet, slowly lifting their shirts. It happened a lot.

When Corey and Pete D. relapsed, they blew a G on rock in a single afternoon. That night's group was normal. For a minute. Guys talked one at a time. Then Pete spoke. He said something else. His tone quickened.

Program's face got screwy. Hey, wait, he said. Motherfucker, have you been smoking rock?

I had to look myself.

Pete's eyes were glazed over. His body shone with sweat. Normally, he wore a suit but tonight had on gym shorts, a white tee, flip-flops.

Yup, he said. Me and Corey. Been at it all afternoon. He smiled at Corey, who looked away. Whatever, bra, Pete said. You weren't ashamed at the time.

Then he got ballsy, I admit, funny but not: he went into some detail over what had happened. Know what else? he said. Fuck you. I can't wait to do it again. When he began talking about the smoke hitting his lungs and how it blew the crown off his head, blew it sky-high, Program lost it. There was no Take two brothers, no Pack your shit, no Ice, nothing, just Get the fuck out my house.

What about my stuff? Pete asked.

Naw, Program said. Get the fuck out.

Pete and Corey were gone.

Guys came and went. I can't put names on all. Like Darryl, they showed up on a Friday, got the drift, and were gone by Monday. Mike W. Chad G. Doug. Brandon. One of the many Andys. At seventeen, I thought of them all as the coolest motherfuckers I'd ever met. Kyle, Will J., Dallas John. Even J-Dog, with his shades and backward hat, who'd once driven his car under the trailer of an eighteen-wheeler and had to have the top of his head sewed back on, is, last I heard, drinking again.

I remember their haircuts, the hats they wore and removed in Group, how they held these hats on their knees or in their laps, Jack Rehab working the brim of his Bulls hat between his thumb and index finger, his scuffed-up Jordans tapping. Andy C. leaned so far back in his chair that he was parallel to the floor, twenty-eyed Docs crossed, hands shoved deep in his pockets. Certain truths unfolded again and again. Carl, from Shreveport, was thirty-four and cocaine-thin, teeth rotted; DOC: crack. He'd been through the House once before, and it wouldn't work this time, either. I have no memory of most brothers leaving. Mark stayed sober as long as I heard updates. Brad P., who once had more Hours than exist in a week, was kicked out for getting gay on another brother on Property. He relapsed, wound up in a psych ward, is dead. Rick K. smoked rock in Room Five and is dead somewhere as well. Some of this, as with the child actor, I don't know for sure. Word of the dead can pile up, get taken on like news, weather, and sports. I know it more from feelings than hard specifics, recalling phone booths in exotic Elko, Nevada, or Pittsfield, Massachusetts, as I moved between here, there, and some other place, in wind, sleet, rain, snow, or sunshine, my coffee cooling on top of the phone booth, a cigarette in my mouth or hand, about to light up, should I light another, is there more news? Do you have more to say? I was very young when I entered the boys' home and then—not three years later—not young at all.

Hostages

RAY suggested we take personal inventory. This was on Super Flats, after we'd performed Majors and Group Funked the Circle K, when we were smoking grits and flicking butts at the cans outside Room Four. Seriously, he said. What's the worst thing y'all ever done? He didn't care. He was just bored. Think it over, he said. Take your time. Ask a brother. He smiled. Why don't you start, Tommy, you Georgia motherfucker. You're probably one of these sheep fuckers, am I right? I hear it works best if they're on a cliff. So they got nowhere to go but back. Or are you the type to put boots on their hooves, slide right in?

Is that how you do it? Jack Rehab asked Ray.

If I have to, Ray admitted. Now, go on, Tommy. I want real, fucked-up shit.

I was so green. What could I say—I stole shit? Christ. I thought of other things: taking that woman's food, or a guy whose ass I'd whooped in Georgia who'd come looking for me with a gun and who got arrested and who scared me so much that when I thought of going back to Georgia, I knew I couldn't—but I didn't have an answer.

Like most fears, it didn't matter.

Sweet Daddy said they used to live in a second-floor flat, and I pictured it above a run-down liquor store, bar, or auto supply place. I saw the grit of his past—dirty snow, barred windows, random trash, and smokeless smokestacks of Gary. I thought of his woman, her toes curled, hands upturned, her laugh. He'd said she chewed the inside of her cheek when deep in thought, and I imagined her this way now, in a coffin. One day he'd gotten home early, unlocked the front door, and walked up their narrow steps. A door on this landing opened into the kitchen, and when he opened this door and stepped inside, he found his woman getting fucked on the kitchen counter. He used hand, mouth, and leg gestures to illustrate the position— her teeth buried in the man's neck, ankles crossed firmly at his lower back. She wore a cotton sundress. Her bare ass slid back and forth on the Formica counter. Panties dangled from her ankle. The man stood, his buttocks exposed, her freshly painted fingernails digging into his back.

What I did, Sweet Daddy said, was stab that motherfucker.

How many times? someone asked.

A lot. Fifteen? Twenty? I might have stabbed that motherfucker *thirty* times. He rolled the butt of a Newport across his lips, removed it from his mouth, packed it against his thumbnail. I stabbed him until I damn near passed out, I was so tired of stabbing.

When Sweet Daddy first began the stabbing, the man expressed outrage, then shock, and finally fear. Sweet Daddy saw it happen, this range of emotions. Dude pulled his dick out and began running around the apartment, trying, it seemed, to get hold of his bearings. Sweet Daddy kept stabbing him. Over and over. He stabbed this guy, he said, until the guy jumped through the living room window fifteen feet to the street below.

Now he stopped talking. He looked at Ray and Timmy D., then his cigarette. He knocked the collected ash into a butt can, touched the cherry to the aluminum, detailing it. He dragged now, chuckled, shaking his head, but it wasn't a proud chuckle and instead seemed full of knowing and empathy. I've never seen a man, he said, run so fast in my damn life.

I wondered what kind of blade, how long, was it serrated? Stupid questions, even for me. The essential actions—the balling and shanking—had happened in a kitchen, a place of many stabbing utensils. He could've pricked this dude with a three-inch paring knife or hooked him with a shish kebab skewer; it didn't matter. His words were measured, slow. He'd thought of the story many, many times. We could tell he'd been deeply affected by the event.

What did you do to your woman? I asked.

He just shook his head. Nothing, he said. I loved her.

Ray went next. It's always this way, always the guy asking who wants to answer. One day he went to a bank, he said, to cash bad paper, but the teller stuck her hand up. Not happening. He gave her his best up from under, complimented her scarf and earrings, but no. She wasn't nasty or mean, just dismissive. He didn't like that. He snapped. He told her he was lying. Her earrings were ugly. Her scarf, too. He didn't know where to begin about her hair. It made him want to puke. And Jesus, he said. Those eyes.

For a while he drove around, angry. And if I find something on that drive, he admitted, someone to roll, someone just scored, things end way different.

But he couldn't find anything. And never stopped thinking of that teller. He hadn't mattered. That's how quick she shot him down. His anger boiled. He was nothing to her. Nothing. He passed a Walmart, unthinking, circled back, stole duct tape, panty hose, a laundry bag. Then he returned to the bank and waited.

When the woman got off work, he pulled the bag over her head, stuffed her in his trunk.

This was in one state, he said, near the state line. A bridge connected the two, and he drove through a valley of farms, passing university towns and former industrial centers, all abandoned and rusted over, and ascended a series of hills and another valley and another set of hills and switchbacks, until arriving at a national forest. It was very late at night. An empty ranger station greeted him at the park's entrance—it was closed for winter, its gate locked. Ray used a rock to free the lock and drove into the woods, continuing until the road was no road at all, just woods. He got out, popped the trunk, pulled the bound and blindfolded woman up, and set her on her feet.

She stood there, legs bent, back stooped. It seemed, he said, she might have been trying to listen or hear, or was thinking about running, but couldn't tell which way to go. He laughed suddenly and then stopped. He had a look on his face. Pure terror.

This was it, I thought. Whatever Ray had left to tell us would surely be the worst. No one could top it. It was a real conversation ender.

Go on, someone said. What happened?

Nothing, he said. I left her there.

*   *   *

CONCERN SWELLED FOR SWEET DADDY. It seemed he didn't want to leave. He wouldn't get a job, refused to make Phase. Program got involved. He came into group one night, clearly upset. Tell you what I know, he told Sweet Daddy. No one goes through my house without getting into *some* shit. What are you hiding?

Sweet Daddy turned in his chair. Me?

Why the fuck ain't you made Phase? Program said.

I haven't found work.

Are you looking?

Sweet Daddy shrugged. What am I supposed to do, flip burgers?

Yup. That's exactly what you're supposed to do, Program said.

Later, after group, Sweet Daddy rolled the tip of a Newport across his lips. We'd all gathered around him, quiet and respectful of his shame.

The fuck, he asked, do I even want with Phase?

That's how you get out, someone said.

I know what's out there, he said.

Well. You can call your woman. Tell her you love her.

She knows I love her.

Maybe she wants to hear you say it.

She don't want to hear from me, he said.

You don't know that.

I'm older than you, Sweet Daddy said, and I do.

But then, I guess, a nearby retirement home called Program and asked if he knew anyone old but not that old, who might like to sit in their lobby and talk with clients, as if one of them. So Sweet Daddy went down there. Pretty soon he made Phase. Once he made Phase, he got on the phone. Once he got on that phone, he never got off. For five days, he did nothing but gab. We'd see him sunrise to midnight, the heels of his side-zipper gators up on the wall, ashes piled beneath his chair, rag on his shoulder, 409 nowhere to be found.

Five days.

Five whole motherfucking days.

At the end of five days, Program came into group, portable phone in hand, looking strangely washed out, gray. His eyes seemed wet, as if he might soon cry or had been crying or was thinking of crying, if crying were something he could do. Dulled somehow, melancholic, lugubrious, he blandly waved the portable phone at Sweet Daddy.

Phone call, he said. For you.

Me? Sweet Daddy asked.

Yeah, Program said. Why don't you take it in the office.

Okay, Sweet Daddy said, and he got up and began shuffling across the floor.

Program set the phone on the bookshelf. And then he did something I'd never seen him do before—when Sweet Daddy got close, he averted his eyes.

Sweet Daddy reached for the phone, but Program told him no, take it in the office, and again, he could not bring himself to look at the man.

Oh, Sweet Daddy said.

And I have wondered about this "oh" for years. Did he know already? Did he think to run, had he considered all the possibilities?

After Sweet Daddy walked outside and shut the door, Program apologized. There was nothing I could do, he said. I've been negotiating all week how they'd handle it. The last thing I wanted was a bunch of cowboys shooting all y'all up.

I heard shouts, then saw uniforms rushing by the window: US Marshals, FBI, DEA, a lot of them, all wearing Kevlar over their fatigues, with bright white or yellow lettering. They carried machine guns. I could just make out the static from their walkie-talkies.

Sweet Daddy killed a cop, Program said. They been tapping his woman's phone for years.

The Edge

I got a job at McDonald's that paid $4.25 an hour. After deductions, I saved $45 a week. When I didn't work, I hung with Mike outside the library. Always we had girls coming around. They'd take his fingers into their mouth, swallow to his last knuckle. What do you think? he'd ask me. Is she talented? He was having fun.

A few front-runners emerged. They had to be wild, gritty. A car was mandatory. We'd ride one in front, one in back, ducking so no one saw us, drive out to the woods or a swamp, or the prairie, lie on the hood, walk the old cypress docks and stare at pylons, the girls cooking pot or crank, all of them more impossibly fucked up than whoever came before. When new brothers enrolled in school, we'd take them with us, have them sign a Negative Contract, all feeling safe with us, each one making some decision that brought them closer and closer to the road again.

One girl had a Bettie Page haircut, stark blue eyes, defined cheekbones. She used to kiss her finger and touch the roof while driving over the tracks. Once she kissed her finger this way and Mike kissed his and they touched each other's fingertips at the roof. I felt uncomfortable, like I'd seen something bad beyond the ordinary of what we were doing here, as if it were one thing to mindlessly bang or pursue banging, but this here, whatever it was, this touching-of-the-finger business, was something else. Later, they disappeared into a field. For a while I sat on the car's hood, this other girl with me, a very small girl. She might have weighed seventy-five pounds. She had one of those southeastern Louisiana names, Boudreaux or Guidry, and she told me about her family: many, many generations all lived in a compound nearby, a very large compound, hundreds of people in her family, maybe more.

The scenario repeated itself. Frequently. After a while Mike got absentminded, distracted, began slacking in his area. He'd crouch down, rag in hand, but never run his rag across the molding. He swept the toilet rim clean but did not discard what came loose. He accumulated Hours. Our conversations suffered. We no longer talked about life after the House. Had no more matched dreams, no more fantasies of far-flung travel to Thailand, Greece, or Antarctica. I took it personal, thought it was about me. He'd decided I wasn't cool, I lacked that thing. But what really happened: Mike O. was in love.

A dude calling himself Cash Money arrived on the scene. I don't remember his real name. No one called him Cash Money, I can assure you. He was seventeen with straight white hair, not unlike Vanilla Ice. I think he came from Florida, maybe. He decided to do school with us but then quit going. A few days later, he moved into this Bettie Page girl's house. Now brothers joked about it. Said where is "Cash Money"? Have you seen "Cash Money"? Always their fingers curled in quotation marks. I felt bad for Mike.

What do you think? I said. Should we go by there, break his legs or something?

He rolled his eyes at first but, after I kept asking, got that old Mike O. smile.

We knew the girl lived in a trailer park on the prairie somewhere near the highway in wet, slumping earth east of the river, and so we went to find the little mousy girl at the library.

Where y'all been? she asked. Who y'all been hanging out with?

It was just too unknown for me to handle. Where's Bettie Page? I asked. Where's that piece of shit Cash Money?

The mousy girl began crying. That's all y'all care about.

I looked at Mike. He looked away.

It doesn't matter, the girl said. They're gone. Went to Florida. Both of them. You'll never see them again.

THE MORNING MIKE TURNED SIXTEEN, I went into his bedroom and pulled his foot, but he refused to get up and we had words. It was the first time we'd had words. His roommate was Jack Rehab, who'd left and come back, and, even though that slight dogleg had lowered his standing in the House, and was something we considered whenever he opened his mouth, he still found occasion to be confrontational.

What the hell are you doing? Rehab asked.

What's it look like?

Let go, Rehab said. Live and let live.

And what now? I asked Mike. What will you do?

Sleep.

Then what?

Get my GED.

Tell him, I told Rehab, but Rehab pushed by me into the bathroom.

There came a stream of piss, some moaning. Then a trickle. Rehab sighed. The trickle gained momentum, grew to full-bore, died completely, and then began again. Jesus, Rehab said. And sure enough, he kept pissing.

Mike smiled at me as we listened. It was funny.

The toilet flushed. Pipes sputtered. Rehab was taking a shower.

Mike, I began, but he cut me off, his smile gone.

I don't care. I'm tired of this. I can't explain it if you don't want to listen. I been in here, one way or another, all my life. You don't know what that's like. It's just inside. You stay inside. You got nothing to look forward to but what the next inside is like. You aren't like me. You take smart classes. You'll go to college and have a job, but not me. I'll be inside. Right here.

It doesn't have to be that way, I told him.

You know what I want. I want to be a grown-up. I want to make my own decisions. I don't want to be told anymore what to do.

It's just pussy, I said.

What's this? Rehab was back, toweling off in the doorway. Have y'all been banging ass at that damn high school? Group, he yelled. Group! Wearing only a towel, he marched up and down the front porch, opening doors and yelling, Group!

Looks like I'm getting up now, Mike said.

In group we did Hats, Rags, and Verbals. I am not who I claim to be. I don't care about you at all. We clapped, said prayers, sat down. Half-dressed junkies with snipes behind their ears, coffee mugs in hand, grumpy, slightly amused, same old shit.

Rehab began. I called this group out of care and concern for Mike O. and Tommy M., who've been banging ass down at the high school.

Brothers seemed impressed, genuinely interested. Several shouted: I support that!

Tommy, Ray said, *really?* This shouldn't be a Care-and-Concern Group, he argued. We should be stroking him.

Guys clapped. Others yawned, bored with it all. Normal day.

Well, I said.

Oh, Rehab said. Sorry. Only Mike's been banging ass. Tommy, I guess, has just been downstroking in the corner.

Right, I said, and got up, signed out. C'mon, Mike. We got school.

I'm not going, he said.

Whatever. I left. Didn't see him all day. No one called. Vic didn't show up. No one told me get back to the Property. When I got home, Ray and Program were huddled by Program's truck. I tried to walk by them. Really did. Head down, eyes elsewhere.

Where the fuck you going? Program asked.

Signing in, I announced. Then I plan to read my Big Book.

Still got your jokes, he said. Come see. When I walked over, he laid hands. This okay?

Sure, I said. Though I didn't want his hand on my shoulder. His hand knew everything.

How do you feel?

Across the road, in a usually vacant lot, a prefab had been dropped on cinder blocks.

Tommy, he said. Look at me. Are you scared?

Yeah.

That's a good thing. Tommy?

Yeah?

Did you see Mike at school today?

No.

Do you usually?

Yes.

Any idea where he might be?

I looked about the Property, saw some of the brothers gathered about the Coke machine, slouching and spitting, chewing their nails and sucking down butts. I could just walk right into the group room, I thought, and out the back door and into the field and woods and beyond. Is he not here? I asked.

Do you think I don't know what goes on at that motherfucking school? As many junkies as I've sent through that place. You think y'all are the first brothers *in my house* to catch a whiff of pussy?

Uh.

His tone shifted from incredulous to instructive. I want to be clear with you. Do you know what I'm saying? About Mike and you?

I mean.

Some pussy is just pussy, Tommy. But some of it is special.

Uh.

Some girls, he said, like fuckups. They're sick, too.

I . . .

And you know what sickies don't do? They don't learn lessons. Normies touch a hot frying pan once, they don't touch it again. Understand me?

. . .

Nod if you hear me.

. . .

Tell me.

I toed the loose pebbles.

It's three-fifteen, he said. You have until Staffing at five to find him. Ray will drive.

RAY WANTED CIGARETTES. Then a cold drink. Outside Circle K, he told me what he knew. Mike had disappeared that morning. Hadn't signed out. Never showed at school. Rehab thought depression. Chad H. reported Mike claiming he'd leave, first opportunity. I'd never heard Mike mention this. Only in the abstract, in that way we all did—this place sucks, or I can't wait to bounce—which didn't need to be said.

Ray suggested McDonald's, a happening place in that town. Girls buzzed around cars filled with boys, dope smoke wafted from the trees. Inside, people wolfed down burgers and fries, sucked their soft drinks. I asked about. Have you seen my buddy? Little guy? Mike?

But no one had.

This girl, Krystal, an assistant manager, came out from behind the counter, brushed against Ray's arm, and walked outside. Ray winked. Then followed her. Andy C. worked the fry station. We made small talk while he turned and burned. Will F. manned the grill. Facedown, sweat dripping off his nose onto the meat. Couldn't or wouldn't scoop, NCs and all. It was 3:40, 3:45. I walked outside. Ray had disappeared. His car was

167

empty. I looked for Krystal's car. I looked in the trees, but the smokers had gone. I went back inside: 3:50. I told Andy to tell Ray I'd be on Magnolia, near the swimming pool.

I began running through the woods. A slight incline led to a narrow creek, and then the land rose. These woods were unlike the rest of southeastern Louisiana—the ground firm, unsaturated. Rocks pushed out from the earth. It reminded me of Georgia, when I used to run through the woods from my house to a friend's, running because I liked the burn of it. I emerged on maybe the only street in town without a gully. A cracked hard curb ran the length of it. A half-block down Magnolia, across from the swimming pool, was a house where the second-prettiest girl in school lived. Slender and big-eyed, with pale skin and delicate wrists, she possessed all the coveted hooks and valleys and would glance up sometimes in fifth-period civics and stare right over my shoulder out the window behind me. She lived in a small brick ranch, nothing extraordinary. Her car in the driveway, flag on her mailbox up, no lights on.

Across the street, Ray leaned against his car, arms crossed, cigarette gritted in his teeth, a curious squint—*are you fucking kidding?*

And he was right. I knew Mike wasn't there. That's the sad part. I just wanted to see this girl one more time before they kicked me out.

She wore a pair of small denim shorts and a pink tank top and greeted me at the door, cordless phone in hand. She couldn't have been more surprised. We'd spoken only once before. In the cafeteria. She'd been playing cards with some friends, and I'd awkwardly asked her what game they were playing. Boo-ray, she said. Is it like spades? I asked. Yes, she said. Then she turned away.

Now she eyed me suspiciously. You're one of those group-home boys, she said, tapping her heel. Well, go on. What do you have to sell me?

I'm wondering have you seen my friend, I said, my hand nipple-high. You know. Guy I'm always hanging out with.

She pointed at Ray. Who's he?

Ray sauntered over. I'm his Big Brother, he announced. Now, where's Mike?

She eyed the ground. I'm—

I need to use your bathroom, Ray said. And your phone. Walking past me, he whispered, Nice try, virgin.

Inside was like every other ranch. They're all the same. Doesn't matter what you do to them. I can walk through blindfolded and drunk and not bump anything. A sliding glass door in the den opened to a small and weathered wooden deck. The backyard had a doghouse but no dog, a clothesline, a plastic kiddie pool. Two lawn chairs faced the pool, one towel, a backpack—not Mike's—a pair of flip-flops, a tube of, I think, tanning cream. There was a cold drink in the grass, something in a glass, the glass sweating, ice melted.

You're just staring, the girl said. Then: You are so weird.

I wanted to say something, but Ray shoved by me, shaking his head. Let me see that phone, he told her.

She stiffened against the sliding glass door, hands clasped behind her.

Yeah. Ray spoke into the phone. The motherfucker went to Magnolia, just like you said. Headed to Prairieville next, I guess. He rolled his eyes at me. I'll call from the Ten.

The road to Prairieville stretched out like all the other country roads around here—lined by pines and cypress, pastures and
swamps, with gullies running along each side of the asphalt. We
passed barns, stables, churches. Puffy cumuli floated below a
soft blue sky. Little details bothered me. Ray had known which
house was hers. He hadn't been at all surprised. He'd mentioned Prairieville. How the fuck did he know about Prairieville?

How are you so dumb? he asked me now.

I guess some things I don't want to see, I said. It was now
4:30. Like, this here. Mike is gone. Right? But. Like. Would
Program send someone after you? Would he send someone
after me?

Everyone's different, he said. You know that.

What does he know?

Everything, he hissed.

Does he know about Krystal?

Ray flipped his fingers at the prairie. Hell, no.

Mike's not coming back, is he?

No.

We drove to a kind of trailer park, only it wasn't so organized. It had no fancy title like Shady Acres or Royal Oaks.
Blocks remained unplotted, roads unpaved. There were no
extras—no pool or community room, no basketball hoop,
seesaw, or swing set. This was not a community of independent
people but offshoots of one family spreading out from some
central ten-wide so that each subsequent structure connected
back to this hub, one trailer running into the next through a
series of corrugated tin roofs, mismatched porches, and cluttered parking areas. We drove slowly through the narrow maze,
peering into the ramshackle and battered homes. Everything

that couldn't fit inside was piled in carports—old refrigerators, stacks of plywood and boards, entertainment centers, children's toys, appliances and TVs that hadn't worked in years, old cars, empty and half-erect chicken coops, reels of barbed wire, wet insulation, rusted oil drums. Dogs pawed and sniffed at the ground, chewed on stacks of tree limbs, or bowed and reared up and barked from inside cramped kennels. A trash pile, maybe ten feet high, burned in a nearby vacant field. An old codger wearing jean shorts and white rubber boots, with stringy hair draping down his shirtless sun-reddened back, stoked its flames.

Any ideas? Ray asked me.

Hell, I said. I don't even know if she lives here.

We stopped in front of one shanty with a couple lanky homeboys sitting on its stoop. One of them was working over a transistor radio with a screwdriver. The other smoked. Ray scratched at his face. I'll get out, he said. I'll ask.

A few more guys came around the trailer's edge. They wore the same outfit the man in the field wore—white shrimpers, cutoffs, no shirt. Black ringed their eyes, stubble shrouded their faces. One of them was carrying a sawed-off.

Ray did not get out. He waved, almost politely, threw the car in reverse. Fuck it, he said. He's not here.

4:50.

It's been real, at least, I said.

Oh, man. Ray grinned. Want me to drop you off here?

We passed a cow pasture darkened by patches of mud. There were pines, a blue sky. An off-yellow ten-wide peeked through the trees. There's a house back there, I said.

Ray squinted. I'm sorry.

All this time I've wanted to leave and now.

You don't want to.

I'm worried.

You should be. This is the safest you'll ever be.

Do you believe that? I asked.

I been here a year, man. And you know what, I'll be here until they make me leave. I'm looking at five years, minimum. Five.

WHEN WE GOT BACK to the Property, Mike O. was sitting in an easy chair in his apartment, staring out the window at the back field, a sad look on his face. I asked where he'd been and he said it didn't matter, and then I asked what was going on with him and he said, Don't start with me.

I crouched beside him, looking at the field, hoping to catch sight of whatever he saw. Remember when we used to talk Iceland and Florida and Texas? I asked. Remember when we used to talk about New York? We can still go there.

That ain't my dream, he said. I'm a caged bird, man. Don't you get that? But I'm not built for cages. I should be free. And I'll never be free.

It seemed melodramatic, over-the-top, a teen's outlook, teen angst, this feeling that the present will always be present, the bad isn't temporary but fixed and life doesn't go on, and yet this was all he knew and had known for a very long time.

How can you, I asked, make it through this?

He turned toward the window again. I can't.

It was the last time we ever spoke.

In group, Program promoted me to the second-highest position of authority in the House: BBG Checker. Then he fired the other BBGs, leaving me to run the place myself. Some guys would've taken this as a compliment and felt good about themselves, but I took it as a warning.

Ask for help, he said.

Afterward, he summoned me to the back porch. I thought to talk about Mike, but he didn't want to talk about Mike. Mike, he said, had a bad day. Bad days happen. And so forth. What are people saying, Program asked me, about this Cookie Monster?

The Cookie Monster was brand-new, three weeks in. He was nineteen, full-blown schizophrenic, drug of choice: PCP. He talked to himself, to bars of soap, tubes of toothpaste, and bottles of shampoo. He'd strut about the Property smoking a cigarette out of each hand. He'd have one tucked behind each ear and loosies rolling about his breast pocket. And yet, straight-faced, he'd bum another. He wore a full beard, had curly brown hair and kind blue eyes. He'd begin laughing suddenly. Out of nowhere. Like in group, when someone was crying. He'd just start laughing. Or he'd talk into his fist. He'd put his fist to his ear and listen. Sometimes, when his fist spoke to him, he'd get mad and argue with his fist, but then wait, hold up, no, it was all a misunderstanding, something to laugh about, actually, a real hoot, and he'd be off cackling again.

I told Program the truth: Motherfuckers are worried.

There's nothing to be worried for, Program said. He's not violent. Just crazy. His voice bubbled with sadness. People like him die young, he said, placing a hand on my shoulder. I'd like him to have a good life while he's still with us.

I HAVE THIS DREAM sometimes where I'm behind the group room with Mike, looking out at the grass and pines, talking about how things will be when we're out, but then the land-scape changes and I'm running through it scared, full speed up the levee, but cresting the levee, rather than the river, I see a swamp below—it's familiar, I know it, been here already, seen it a hundred times—with cypress knees and alligators sloshing about and herons in their cool poses all glancing disparagingly at me. The only way across this swamp is to jump from stump to stump as if I'm in a video game, but the boscoyos teem with water moccasins, a lot of them, slithering, wrapping around each other, pulling tighter, hissing, snapping their jaws. I don't care. I keep running. I run down the levee to the swamp's edge and hop stump to stump, each landing taking me closer and closer to the vipers' fangs. It's so literal. So one-to-one. If I made it up, you wouldn't believe me.

I've had this dream twenty years plus now. A long time.

And I ask you now: Do you need the rundown? Should I say the end? Is there any mystery what happens? If you drove the same road every day to work, would you imagine one day, in a place where you've only ever seen woods, there might this day be a meadow?

A few months later, the Cookie Monster walked into a South Dallas shopping mall with a machine gun and went full auto.

As for Mike O.: he left. So did Ray. They left with Jon B. and Chad H. in Ray's car, a blue Ford Probe. Chad rode shotgun. Ray steered forearm only, cigarette in hand. Jon sat wheel-side backseat, Mike next to him. They headed the wrong way down West Road, and both looked back at the Property once, sloppy grins on their boyish faces. They possessed a few belongings—a change of underwear, some T-shirts, not much.

It was spur-of-the-moment. They'd only just that morning said definitively, You know what, fuck it.

Later, they filled Ray's cars with two slide-action .25s, a pair of twelve-gauges, both with pistol grip, a revolver, a few boxes of ammo. They bought a pound of weed, an eight ball, a case of forties, a couple handles of vodka, some brown liquor, the essentials.

They merged southbound onto I-10, passed NOLA without incident.

In Florida, they began knocking off liquor and convenience stores. They began in the Panhandle, meandered south along the coast, hitting random towns here and there. Ray drove, Mike O. handled the gunplay. They briefly retired in the Florida Keys, fished, fucked pussy, grew restless, bored, got back in the car, began ripping and robbing again. Northbound, they encountered the law. Lawyers called Program. Program knew people. The district attorney owed a favor from back in the day. The boys got a liberal judge. This judge gave them an option—either return to the House or serve hard time. Jon and Ray chose to return to the House. Chad and Mike did not.

Three years later, on November 15, 1998, Mike died. I've no idea how. Don't know where he was living by this time. That spring, in northeast Ohio, law enforcement had arrested someone of the same name and age for B&E, but beyond that, other than this date, his trail is cold. There is no one to call and ask. By then all of us were gone. Even Program had quit working at the House.

Calling

FROM repetition, things began sinking in. I recall no epiph-
any. At some point, it just became clear. After making Phase,
I called my mom and asked was it true.

I'm not sure, she said, why you're even asking.

Not ever? Like even if I finish? You'll never let me back?

You should talk to the group about this, she said.

The group? No, thanks.

If you talk to me about it again, she warned, I'll call Program.
What would he say about you wanting to come back here?

I called my dad. What do you think about me coming out
there, staying awhile, living with you?

Oh, he said, huh. Is that . . . ? Jesus, son. Well, I, I—I don't
know.

Man, I'm trying to get to college, I said.

You'll go when you go, he said. There's no time limit.

But, I said. You.

He was quiet.

Wouldn't it be nice, I said. I look after you, we get to know
each other.

How much longer is the program?

I don't know—six months?

That's nothing.

But in six months—

ON STRICTS OR FLATS, I worried. What if he needs to get ahold of me? I'd walk into the group room and look at the phone. The glorious phone. Is the ringer even on? I'd come home from school and see Program, tell him my concerns, and he'd scratch at his goatee or lay hands on my shoulders. Look at me, he'd say. Are you thinking of going out there? Is that what this is about?

Boss, I'd say. Just boss.

What could he say? Some things just are. He'd point at the phone and leave. I'd call California, ask the old man to tell me about it, and he'd go over it again. According to him, his picture had once been on the cover of *Vogue*.

Fucking-A *Vogue,* son. The cover. I'm going to find that magazine. I'll send it to you. I'll find that magazine.

He described again and again his education at those fancy schools, all of his classmates fancy people, future presidents, a lot of them, owners of large grocery store chains and Major League Baseball teams or they didn't work at all, descendants of Williams and Bradford, Goodman and *Mayflower* who lived in mansions acres and acres from the road. They owned horses, horse stables, they ran horses.

This is what I wanted, all I wanted from him: to know his life had meaning. Tell me about the picture again, I'd say. Tell me about the airplanes you flew. The space shuttles. Tell me how great you are. Mention the famous people you know. And what about your time in the navy?

Well, he'd say, hold on. I've got some of this written down.

Or we got down on the nitty. He was doing okay. Tired, but still kicking. Most his generation dead or about to be. Whole neighborhoods, entire cities eviscerated, gone. The Castro, West Hollywood, P-town, the Village. He could visit now and not know anyone.

I had questions. What about so-and-so? Were you ever in love? What about the dude that day? On the drive? What happened to him?

Dead. Dead. Died last year. Dead. Dying.

Do you visit him?

I did visit him. In hospice.

Good, I said.

His day-to-day consisted of pills and hospitals, blood work, doctors, nurses, tubes, injections, acupuncture, all of it futile. He was tired. He lacked energy, couldn't keep food down. He'd lost weight. There were holes in his face, giant holes. He could stick a Q-tip through these holes, swab his gums. His teeth had rotted, he ground and cracked those rotting teeth. He had permanents, dentures, his facial structure had changed. I'm all eye sockets now, he said, just cheekbones. He mentioned specific drugs, specific medicine and doctors. He was still six foot two but weighed only 110 pounds.

When he had the energy, he told me, he meditated or went to hospice to sit with the men. He read a lot. He was learning Cantonese.

Are you smoking?

Sometimes. I mean. I shouldn't, but.

What does Grampa say?

He just. Nothing. He loves me.

And your brother?

Yeah, my brother. He's worried. What about your brother?

He's good.

And the other?

Same.

Will you tell them?

What do you want me to tell them?

I don't know, he said. What do they feed y'all there?

Shit.

I bet. Okra? Red beans?

Yeah, yeah. Red beans. A lot of red beans. Red beans and red beans, you know.

Sure. Stuff's good.

Hot buns.

Mmm.

Loads of butter. It's okay.

School?

It's, you know.

What are you taking?

English. I don't know.

History? What are they teaching you in history?

Stuff.

Math? Science?

Yeah. I don't know, though.

Is it a. I mean. Pretty good school?

No.

Well. Focus. Finish. You got a long life ahead of you.

Sleepless, I'd listen to my roommate breathing or what-ever strange mumbling came from the front bedroom of our apartment. Every night, I hoped for rain. When it rained now, I couldn't hear things. I didn't think. It was just rain then. Rain reminds me of home, of Georgia. How hot it was, how I could never sleep as a kid. Only when it rained.

When I slept, I slept lightly, in fits and lucid dreams. I'd wake before my roommate and stumble to the group room to check the board for word of a missed call. Then I'd make coffee and stare out at the field. Soon my dad would call, or someone else, maybe my grampa. Did he have my number? Did my dad? My mom had moved again. She had a new phone line. How would anyone get ahold of me so I'd know?

Vic woke me. Fucking Vic. He had this horrible cackle of a laugh. He'd randomly come up to you—he did this to everyone—and laugh. He always had a joke.

Later—I'm talking years, like gray-hairs-on-my-head later, when I was for sure washed up completely—I'd stop by late at night, feeling completely empty, and find him half-asleep in the office, *SportsCenter* blaring on the TV, a Big Gulp sweating on a copy of the Big Book on the coffee table next to him. We'd get to talking about this and that. What do you hear from Morning Wood? he'd ask. He still with old what's-her-face? You know what they say, Vic, he'd tell me, two sickies a wellie don't make.

He was the worst driver ever, yet drove us everywhere. This was another of Staff's gags, a practice in letting go, acceptance, trust in God. He'd dart through clogged roads as if his were the only car, rabbit into oncoming traffic to pass a truck, or speed by in the breakdown lane, always talking and looking at us and never the road. No matter how much you want to know, we'd warn new brothers, close your eyes, put your head down. DO NOT LOOK.

It was five a.m. when he woke me. Vic? I said.

Vic, he said, handing me the phone. It's your dad.

I looked at the phone. Let me get dressed, I said. Let me find a cigarette.

He pushed his glasses up his nose. No joking now. I'll be outside, he said, if you need me.

In the South, it gets so hot and muggy you can't get off the front porch. Even after the mailman comes, and you've waved, it's not worth what crossing the yard requires. Closing your eyes, you see stars, feel light-headed, a need to sit down. But it was early still; there was moisture, a dampness in the pines. On the horizon, over Pontchartrain, clouds churned in layered navy, charcoal, heather, and black. A storm was coming in from the gulf. Lightning slipped down, slipped back up.

Dad, I said. Sorry I haven't called. We're on Flats again.

He was brief, exact. I'm going into hospice today.

It's hard to admit how naïve I was, but I didn't know what he meant by saying, "I'm going into hospice today." Not really. I thought he meant that he was going to volunteer, look after one of his friends.

Son, he said, are you there? Did you hear me?

How long will you be there? I asked.

A few days? I don't know. A week, tops.

It seemed like a long time to volunteer, and yet I wanted to understand what all this death was like. He wanted to sit with his friend. A week is nothing for someone you love.

Well, call me in a week, I said.

For a while, he didn't speak. Pine straw had shaken loose in the night and cluttered the back slab. I'd have to clean this soon, or someone would. I took long drags of my cigarette. Birds made haunted noises like they will before a storm: shallow calls, small, not bellicose or musical but little, and of warning, wings fluttering in their nests.

Dad, I said. Can you call me in a week?

I can only wonder what he felt. Frustration? Relief? His side of the street was clean. He'd called and given me the news. What more could he do?

Okay, he said. Call you in a week, I guess.

I CAUGHT SOME long stares that week. A lot of brothers palmed my back or shoulders. I'm okay, I told them. Don't worry. He'll call in a few days, a week, tops.

After a few days, I began wondering. I couldn't eat. Instead I'd smoke another cigarette or drink more coffee, get more and more jittery, less and less hungry. I asked Program could I call. He gave me this look like Huh, say what? But must have thought better of questioning me. Sure, he shrugged. Go ahead. I'll be in the kitchen.

I left messages. Hey. It's me. Just checking in. Wondering how you're doing. Hope you're okay. Thinking of you. Let me know what's up. Are you okay?

Two weeks passed. No one called to talk about any funeral or wake. No one called, period. Not my mom. Not anyone who knew my dad. The weeks became a month. No word. We went off Flats and back on. I kept calling. Calling and leaving messages. Calling and hanging up before the answering machine came on. Hanging up and calling again. Calling and calling and calling. No one corrected me. No one said, Knock it off, you can hang up now, he won't answer, that man is dead.

The baseball coach called the House. Legion tryouts, Friday. It barely registered. Nothing I could do on Flats. No way. But Ray and a few brothers pitched Program: What if we Group Funk it? Program smiled. Guys pulled on their cleanest wifebeaters, gelled their hair, spit-smoothed their eyebrows. You can imagine the scene—twenty-four junkies, butts hanging from their mouths, chain-wallets swinging by their legs, stepping between eager parents and their small offspring—as the whole House, minus me, ascended from the bleachers. I'd expected them to ditch out, rampage across campus turning over trash cans and emptying lockers in search of young snatch, but no one left. From the diamond, I watched them. Could tell by whose lips moved, and how quickly, the kind of shit they were talking. They catcalled and whistled. They chanted my name. It didn't matter if I booted grounders or airmailed relays, they cheered, stomped their feet. Nice try, chin up, good throw. I stepped in the box. Their stomping intensified. The pitcher stepped off the rubber. He took a deep breath, removed his hat, and wiped his brow. The catcher rose from his crouch and stood next to me. I didn't want to be at the plate anymore. I wanted to be with my brothers.

Are you okay? the catcher asked.

Yes, I said, blinking.

Are you sure?

Yeah. It's just. There's something in my eye.

Calling

WHEN I GOT HOME, a strange feeling came over me, almost ghostlike. As if hovering, I saw from both my own eyes and someone else's, could see myself sign in, check the board for messages, pass through the group room to the backyard. It was eighty-five, sunny, a slight breeze from the southeast. Insects. A hummingbird lowered from the sky and hovered over some florets as they nodded in the wind. What I thought: I can die. It was clear, concise; a realization: I could kill myself. Nothing ever has to be bad. There's a way to make the pain stop.

I felt at peace. And from my serenity, a clarity emerged. As dumb as I was, I knew I had to move on.

Program was in the office. I told him my plans.

Call group, at least, he said. Meanwhile—you know the drill. Take two brothers and pack your shit.

Ray volunteered. And E-Dog. But I couldn't pack. I sat on my bed, watched Ray breeze through my things. We bartered over a pair of pants and some sneakers, settled on bad deals designed to put me ahead a few bucks.

Where you going, anyway? Ray asked. Where the fuck does a bastard go? It's sad, really. He tossed my mitt on the floor and a ball rolled out. There's nothing out there, he said. What will you do when you find that out? Will you come back? 'Cause you got nowhere, really. Nowhere at all.

Same thing got said in group. Didn't change a thing. I slept in my clothes in the group room corner.

Program woke me, early. What do you need? he asked.

I need to leave, I said.

That's fine, he said. Get the fuck off my Property.

HALFWAY

*   *   *

WALKING DOWN WEST ROAD, I thought of this story my mom told me about some flowers that grow on the prairie. These flowers are only a few feet tall, but they have really long roots, she said, sometimes forty or fifty feet. It's because of water. Prairies are arid. These roots keep growing, looking for water. And I was thinking of these flowers, thinking of what my mom had said, how their roots grow, how they keep searching for water. That was the thing now. I was thinking about flowers.

Year-Rounders

I developed an absolute radar for the absurd, the curious, the strange. A week after running away from the House, I found myself in a car and then on a train and then on the side of a highway in upstate New York, walking east toward the state line and mountains. I walked for a long time toward those mountains. I carried a gallon-jug of water and wore an overstuffed hiking backpack I'd stolen from the boys' home. Tied to this backpack was my baseball bat.

The road curved and fell and rose again as it wound over the humped land. Somewhere on this road was a small town with the Farm of the Message. Somewhere. I knew the town was thirty miles from Albany but didn't know where in town the commune was. I figured I'd ask around when I got there.

The highway followed the land up one hill and down the next, coming into and out of many small towns. From a hilltop, I'd see scattered farms, windbreaks, a water tower. Each of these towns had their own chamber of commerce, their own high school, and civic pride; they were all places people came from or stayed in or ended up at. I continued marching on, stomping along the shoulder, left arm extended, thumb up. No one stopped.

For hours, my excitement dulled the shit of walking, muting the humidity, beautifying the ordinary. I was alone, with no one to report to, and happy. I believed in fate, in God's will—each passing car wasn't the right ride, its driver the wrong companion. I needed to be on this road, trudging along. Nothing discouraged me. My quads burned, my calves cramped, a dryness cracked my throat, and I felt grateful. I can be stubborn, dumb. Cresting a hill after twenty-odd miles, I came to a deep turnout with views of the valley ahead and valley behind, the scant snake of asphalt in trees. A low sun cast shadows over the next valley of spotted fields, barns, and new rows of corn. A wooded ridge rose in the distance, miles away. The commune was on that ridge. Overgrown foliage had created a bowl at one of the turnout, shielded from the road. I dropped my bag, guzzled water. Then I shook loose a cigarette, and considered this foliage. It was a place to sleep, maybe, but also a place of privacy, for prey, a place to wait—a predator's dream. I walked back to the highway's edge. In the valley below, a car raced through the buckled farmland until it disappeared in trees. It reappeared and disappeared again, climbing the hill toward me. When I saw it again, I stuck my thumb out.

It slowed long before reaching me, as if the driver was considering the proposition, and, in its approach, I began expecting the ordinary—the car would drift to the side of the road and stop, I'd get in, and we'd be off. Instead, it passed by me and pulled into the turnabout, before circling back. It was a piece-of-shit car. The kind you can steal easy or buy for a few hundred bucks. American-built, four doors, faded maroon.

A man got out. Maybe six foot one, and thin, he wore gray slacks, had salty brown hair, glasses. Scattered gray stubble sparkled against his reddened cheeks. He had that look like he'd been drinking, maybe, or the last few days had been unkind, and he sort of stared at my T-shirt, a faded yellow thing with "Gonzales" written on it.

What is Gonzales? he asked.

A town.

Where?

Louisiana.

Is that where you're from?

No.

Is that where your parents live?

I'm looking for a ride, I said.

It's just a town?

That's right.

And you have this town written on your T-shirt?

I couldn't read his license plate but saw into a backseat papered with flyers. Someone had stapled his roof upholstery, but it had come unstapled and hung loose in places above the seats. There was a pair of binoculars on the dash.

It's just a shirt, I told him.

That's my name, he said. I'm Officer Gonzales. When I didn't acknowledge this, he told me it was illegal to hitchhike in New York.

I wasn't hitchhiking, I told him, smiling.

I passed you a while back, he said. And turned around. Now he smiled.

He was not the kind of guy you wanted smiling at you like that.

Don't want anyone getting abducted out here, he said. Don't want anyone getting in a car with someone and killing them or anything. Happens around here all the time. I'm police, he added, but he didn't look like police and didn't show me a badge. Where are you headed?

I told him.

Is that where you live?

Where I'm going to live.

You moving there?

I didn't answer.

How old are you?

What's all this about? I asked.

Are you a runaway?

No.

He stepped toward me. Then stepped again, each step barely perceivable, until he stood an arm's length away. I'll have to see your ID, he said. I'll have to run it, see if you're a runaway. If you are a runaway, I'm going to arrest you.

His old beater was no cop's ride. How are you going to "run" my ID? I asked. You got a CB in there? Or something?

What's your name?

I told him the truth.

Spell it, he said.

I started spelling it, but he got that creepy grin on his face, and I began backing up toward my bag. As I stepped back, he stepped forward. He was sure-footed, cocky. I watched his hands and hips, the width of his gait, the emphasis of his footfall, looking for a chance to run.

Where are you going? he asked.

I'm getting my ID.

His eyes shifted from me to my bag. Is that a baseball bat?

I smiled. Yeah.

Why do you have a bat?

I play baseball, I said, though in saying it, I knew it wasn't true anymore—baseball was something I used to play when I was a child, and I wasn't a child now. I looked up, hoping to convey this new understanding of things, but his posture had changed, his cockiness had all worn off. He began to lecture me, but not slow and steady, as he'd been all this time, and instead, hurried and scared—You'll never catch a ride carrying a baseball bat, it's spooky, how dare you, etc. He got in his car and sped off.

I admit it: I tossed my bat into the foliage. The dude was right. The next car picked me up.

LATER, I WALKED UP a steep hill past orchards and fields and Shaker buildings, and eventually, the road turned to gravel and there were more Shaker buildings, a cluster of them, and a barn and an old green house and some weather-beaten VWs. The guru was gone. Most of the businesses and people, too. Now it was just a few old-timers, their long hair tied in pony-tails, Birkenstocks worn through at the treads.

I moved into a small room not unlike the room I'd shared with Lee and my mom all those years ago. I worked on the farm, strutting about shirtless, wearing cutoff fatigues and steel-toed boots. I started carrying a large hunting knife with a bored-out blade you could pull quickly from a hump of flesh, a real killing knife—no one was pulling my wrists through a banister now—and came and went, free. These were experiential days, each of them new, each offering another beginning, as if I'd been born again, as all my actions placed me on the cusp of recovering something that I probably never had. They were the kind of days where you'll get in a car and go somewhere or jump in some water and swim without thinking and then you look up and there's a snake or bear or a forest ranger, or you repose on a soft hill of fine fescue watching the sun slip over some pastoral fantasy of cows and red barns and hard work, where coffee tastes bolder, vegetables fresher, songbirds sing sweeter, fireflies shine brighter, and there are other run-aways and dropouts around who aren't junkies but good kids, smart, who merely foresaw the joke's end and decided to do something different and follow the harvest from California, Florida, and Arizona, detasseling corn, picking blueberries, and chopping onions, their hair long and beards patchy, potato eaters and vegans, singers and painters, communal dwellers.

Was this how my mother had felt way back in 1970-whatever?

Everything seemed important, everything possessed meaning; no matter how small or inconsequential—cool water, blue skies, a dock in the middle of a pond, a girl in a bikini, rain, thunder, lightning. One day my friend Cody and I were sprawled in the grass on a mountain road, lying on our laundry bags, smoking cigarettes, when a minivan pulled up and two girls leaned out the window and we spoke to them and they conferred and, in conference, stole a glance—wish I had a picture of it—looking at us and then each other, this smile between them, a real sweet smile, not saccharine or over-the-top but sweet, a couple girls smiling sweetly over some boys.

That summer was all about summer. It was about eating processed pork off a stick. It was about water, swimming in it and drinking it. It was about hiking, or balancing on a single railroad track, the way silt at the bottom of a river feels between your toes. It was about cars, moonlight, fireworks, peanuts, cotton candy, chili cheese fries, and strawberry milk shakes. It was about how warm a bonfire feels when it is raining. And then one night—there is *always* that one damn night—one of these girls pulled my face close to her own. C'mon, she whispered. And would I need my boots, I asked, but she didn't answer, just led me from that fire and into the woods, and we walked for a long while through these woods until we came to a clearing with tall grass and a hill, and we made our way up the hill and lay down in the grass and it was done.

The next day, I called my dad's phone. I'd been calling a lot still. Maybe not every day, but often. Usually, I'd just let the thing ring a while and then hang up, but today I aimed to leave a message. I wanted to tell him what had happened. But something strange occurred: he picked up.

You're okay, I said.

I'm fine.

I've been calling.

I know.

So, I said.

Yeah.

You haven't called, I said. What happened?

I've been busy.

Busy.

There's been some controversy, he said.

With?

Son, I can't talk about it now.

But talk about it he did. He went on to suggest all manner of nonsense—investigations, double and triple homicides—not to mention there'd been a lot of calls to return, a lot of things to deal with, and so it went, nothing personal.

And in the end, I didn't care about these stories. I was just glad he was alive.

THE SUMMER WORE ON to August, and I left for Cape Cod, where I hitchhiked around a bit. I had vague plans of going west and then returning. That's what I told the girl. I'll be back. I wanted to work the harvest on the commune, then go to New Mexico, where my bio dad said he'd be. I was just going to travel now. That was the plan. I had my backpack, my big knife, some matches, a few hundred bucks.

One afternoon, stranded outside a convenience store, I watched the endless summer people come into and out of this place with their station wagons and minivans brimming with coolers and folding chairs, kayaks and such strapped to their roofs. They gassed up, stretched, got back in their cars, and headed west. There was the commotion of children and dogs and exhausted parents, sunbaked, sweating oils and liquor and sugar, all sleepy-eyed and dreamlike, ready to be home.

A Nova pulled in. Two women, one pretty. The Nova was all beat to hell. They parked next to an air compressor and got out and sat on their hood and looked nervously at the road full of cars. One of them stood and began pacing. They spoke frantically with their hands or buried their faces in their hands or chewed skin off their hands. A car of teenage boys showed up, and the pretty one walked over and peered in the window and shook her head. Next was my turn. She slithered over and asked to see my fingernails.

I showed her, but she turned her nose. So I went inside, found a bathroom, freshened my areas.

I guess she never found anyone better or had forgotten me altogether. When I returned, she eyed me with renewed interest. Here he comes now, she announced. Jack Kerouac himself.

That's right, I said. Now I'd like to read you a poem if you'll let me.

She was kind of flirty—the better-looking of the two—but the other one just said, That's fine, let's go.

I'd like to say I didn't think about it, but that's not true—I did think about it. Both too taut and jerky, they grinded their jaws and moved too slow. They had the feel of the victim— someone had done them wrong, and now someone would pay. And someone *had* done them wrong: purple-eyed, with a darkened cheek, the driver slurred through a busted lip and a chipped front tooth. She needed dental work, a damp compress, some TLC. She seemed a few years older than me. Both did. They were busted in a pharmaceutical way, with loose skin and coon eyes, all self-will, determination, and fuck you, and though I kept seeing the image of the one pacing back and forth angrily, I got that same stubborn thing myself—when I want something, I just don't care.

I sat behind the driver, my bag beside me, but the driver turned and barked for me to sit bitch. She wanted to see me.

I thought it was a come-on and moved to the middle of the backseat.

The passenger leaned back and rolled her head, her sharp lips and mouth close to mine, her breath hoppy and sour. Do you party? she asked.

I like to have fun, I said, though I knew what she was asking, and this wasn't an answer to that question.

We're looking to party, she told me.

She was slinky, with defined limbs, her hair tied up, while the driver was kind of tall and built for hard use. Her hair lifted in the wind.

Empty cans of beer and cigarette packs littered the backseat. A discarded Filet-O-Fish wrapper got caught up in the breeze and sucked out the window. Behind me hung a clothesline with panties and crop tops. The girls wore little more than that—both had on bikini tops and cutoff shorts. They'd been at this whole summer thing awhile.

So, the driver asked. What are you doing later?

I had no idea. None. I could see, like I said, a few months down the line, returning to the commune for harvest, going west, but I was all out of concrete plans.

We'll be in Plymouth, one of them announced.

I could meet y'all there, I said.

Oh, the passenger said, do you party?

She was so strung out.

A rusted crowbar, splotched with blood or red or brown paint, rested between her legs.

Jesus, I said, noticing it, half question, really.

She turned in her seat, her knees to its back, and reached behind her head, pulling free whatever had been tying her hair up. It was a small, short-handled stabbing knife or dagger, and she held it now as if to stick me.

The crowbar, she said, is for you.

Hey, the driver said. Then she said something else, but I couldn't hear it. They both watched me in the rearview but inched closer together, their mouths almost touching as they whispered and shook their heads. I strained to listen but only heard hissing. Just hissing. Their lips peeled back, tongues darting in and out, the driver hissing and nodding and the passenger shaking her head. Then I heard the words "plan" and "talked" and "about" and "do" and "him." I heard "him" quite a few times.

CAPE COD IS A THIN STRIP OF LAND jutting first east and then north into the Atlantic. On a map, it looks like a bent arm and a hand making a fist. It's a summer place. Homes here are built for the summer. Some don't have much in the way of insulation, lack heaters—a lot of them don't even have full baths, just shower stalls. There are many towns, all of them small enclaves of summer cottages, summer churches, ice cream and hot dog stands. In the summer, their populations might reach fifty or sixty thousand but, in the winter, dwindle to just a few hundred people; motels and cafés and restaurants get boarded up, and there is nothing but wind, sand, and coyotes. The eastern coyote is very different from a western coyote. They're larger, more aggressive—a result of hybrid DNA. Somewhere along the way, they bred with wolves.

We were driving down a highway bordered by woods. I knew on either side of these woods would be frontage roads and cottages and then the ocean to the south and Massachusetts Bay to the north. I know when I talk about this place, it's hard not to see privilege: I imagine a Kennedy finger-blasting a caterer in the shadows of a party tent, a splotch of cum on white linen pants, lipstick on the rim of a champagne flute, but it isn't like that for everyone. Like the caterer. Some people have to keep moving. Even after all the decisions they've made are wrong, they still have to keep going, even after summer ends.

Listen, I told these girls, wait. I'm not holding.

Los Angeles

No telling how all I got around. In truck beds and backseats, on buses and trains, ferries and planes. There were commuter lines and light rails, locals and expresses, all of it lobbied for or arranged by a friend of a friend. I'm quite sure I tobogganed across western Colorado. Here is the truth, and hold on to your asses, people, because it's always the truth: back in California, I met a girl I loved so much I knew I'd have to leave town or start drinking again.

I was young. And even before we got together, I'd drive thirty and forty minutes out of my way to places I thought she might be, hoping to catch sight of her automobile. I worked across the street from her high school at a grocery store, and sometimes she'd come in with her mother and I'd take my time bagging their few items, hoping to say something, always so runny-feeling and jumpy, and after they'd leave, I'd go to the loading dock with a coworker and we'd climb onto the roof and talk about our feelings. One day, I convinced her to get in a car with me. We drove to Reno. After that, we began exploring California, and we drove into the San Joaquin and Mojave and all up and down the PCH, stopping at roadside fruit stands or wandering out into a patch of strawberries or up a mountainside; once I lost her in Grass Valley for a few days but found her in a patch of woods east of Nevada City.

Her name was Sally Kaplan and she was nineteen years old. She had layered and straight, long blonde hair, a tight ass, the most incredible legs. We were so sweet together it was senseless. She wore this bright red trench coat and I'd hold her by its belt. It's not even worth explaining.

Eventually, she got a scholarship to study dance at a university in Los Angeles. I still recall the promises we made the night we cashed her college money and rolled it into socks we tucked away in a drawer at our small apartment. This money would last until we ran away together and had kids.

But things began changing for me. I stopped eating, stopped sleeping. I stopped exercising. I stopped talking about my dark thoughts. You can believe anything you want when you don't seek outside counsel. Fears became stories verified by further stories leading to resentments leading to more of the same. Put another way: I stopped making amends and instead went looking for apologies.

WE RENTED A fifteen-by-fifteen-foot room in a ten-story co-op on top of a hill. We had no kitchen or faucet, no microwave or hot pot; we shared a bathroom down the hall with several other rooms. Sally was gone all day at class and all evening in rehearsal, and by the time she got home, I made it a point to be gone myself.

Some days I'd drive as far as Palm Springs, where I'd sit with my dad for a while with our cigarettes and coffee and what I thought was a mutual curiosity but wasn't mutual at all. He liked talking about himself. And he was lonely. He told fanciful tales involving off-color humor and wild mystery—they always offered the same hero and often forgot themselves. He no longer claimed a murder investigation had prevented him from contacting me after he survived hospice but much worse: he'd been on the lam, he said, many, many years. He wasn't a criminal, no. Someone was chasing him. There was a lot of talk about the many times he'd disappeared, all of it from him. He'd moved someone into his home, he suggested, but that someone had drowned in a swimming pool.

When was that? I asked.

Oh, he said. That summer. Six months or so after the hospice.

He had no idea how long he had now.

I was barely holding on, myself. In every situation, I looked for something different and new to feel in the midst of shit again. Odd things excited me. A neighbor lady used to whisk past my apartment in zebra-patterned leggings. I'd hear her whispering thighs from my desk and quit my game of solitaire, get up, follow that wonderfully erotic whooshing down the stairs, through the lobby, and onto the hill, where, cloak-and-dagger, I'd trail her into town. And where was she going? What sort of feelings did she possess? Did we speak? Did she notice me creeping? Did she care? I lacked direction, perspective, motivation, friendship, protein, calories, etc. In Rite Aid or some liquor store, I'd linger by the magazine rack for hours. My sleep suffered. Awake two, three days straight, I slowed physically, my pace stalled, my brain, my speech, the way I processed information; I had visions, saw tracers, glowing lights, people falling from buildings—hallucinations, all. I'd get home and go to the roof, stand at its edge, and consider the ten-flight drop to the courtyard below where Sally parked her bike—Would she be the one to find my body if I jumped? The eastern sky a strange white-cherry din, I knew she'd be showering now, washing and conditioning her long blonde hair. Soon she'd wrap that hair in a towel, wrap her body in another towel, gather her shower supplies, and head back to our room, where she'd sit on our bed, a foot up, rubbing lotion into her skin. She had a beautiful voice and liked to sing, and I imagined her in these moments humming a tune she always hummed about migrant workers in central California, men and women who'd always wanted something else but knew the road was long, dreary, and full of things you'd never expect. She'd dress slowly—socks, then chonies and bra, taking her time, applying eyeliner, lipstick, in case I came home. The whole idea of her purposefully taking her time so she could be there for me made me crazier and crazier, and I'd sit at the roof's edge, dangling my legs, hoping the wind might pick up or someone would come from behind and pat me too hard on the back. Sometimes I'd sleep, and when I slept I'd sleep for days on end and maybe I would've disappeared completely, as a directionless young man will disappear sometimes, literally he'll drop off the face of the earth, only to be rediscovered under an overpass or at a city shelter, except early that November, after the rains came, a serial rapist arrived on campus.

Well, hello, I told Sally, folding the paper neatly. How interesting.

She wore some kind of crotchless lace—I don't know what it's called—and, prancing about in front of me, she practiced a few of her dance moves, prodding me with the usual Do you like? and then Is there something wrong?

It seems, I said, there's some douchebag running around.

She began sashaying toward me but, Hold on, I told her, be right back, and I slid from bed and into some jeans, shoed my sneakers. It was ten, maybe eleven p.m., and I walked down the hallway and then the stairwell and into the lobby and through the double doors and down the steep hill to the main college drag. Every hundred yards or so, stapled to a telephone pole or light post, I found another sketch of the rapist's face. The man had a familiar look, okay, the kind a lot of guys wore that year: bold eyes, a goatee, long-ass sideburns. In most he wore a skullcap or baseball hat. The flyers listed him six-three or so, 180 pounds, more or less what I was carrying in those days.

I looked in shadows and alleys, behind grocery stores and SUVs, loitered about bus stops and under eaves. I found myself eyeballing every man who waited outside the various fast-food eateries and bars on the main drag. I walked the entirety of the campus, cased every floor of every building, every nook, aisle, and private study area in the library, popped into and out of several bathroom stalls, lingered around research facilities, pressed my face to the glass of math and science labs. Finally, I saw a tall, thin man emerging from trees on a quiet road housing the sororities, but he eluded me, and then, after I was all walked out, I saw him again, standing in the shrubbery outside our building.

What's this? I said. Who the hell are you?

Oh, thank God, he replied. Have you got a match?

He was my height, at least, or maybe shorter, and wore a mechanic's coat; wet jeans clung to his bony legs.

I pulled out my lighter. Do you live here?

I've seen you many, many times. He pointed to the rainy sky and roof. Up there.

Yes, I admitted. You can find me up there a lot these days.

You're with that girl, he said, his long eyelashes blinking under his skullcap. He had a light blond beard that hadn't grown in all the way around his mouth, and eyes dulled and darkened by Percocet. She's pretty.

I started to respond, but he cut me off, explaining he drove a taxi, which seemed dubious, and then he said he used to live in the desert near Joshua Tree, but I didn't believe that, either. His truth was as apparent as my own—we both lived in this co-op and both viewed the world through a certain scope: when we saw red flags, instead of running away, we moved forward.

So, he said, as you can see, I know most everything that goes on around here. My name's Brian.

What are you doing in L.A.? I asked.

Just living the dream.

I nodded. I, too, was living a sort of dream.

Come here, he said. Come in out of that rain. What do they call you?

Close in among the shrubs, I saw where his wet fingers had pulled his cigarette apart. This was not my guy, I thought, but maybe.

And then something unspoken occurred between us. It was the kind of thing that will make the hairs on your neck tingle and your whole body tremble, and the next thing you know, you're somewhere else. I've heard these barroom prophets bragging on various philosophies, how things happen in threes and so forth, but this has never been the case for me. For me, shit always happens in twos or never at all.

You're looking for something, he said. Or someone. I'll take you there.

Here I was, armed with all the self-knowledge in the world, prepared by Program and the others for just this sort of thing, but, like when I got in the car with the pilled-up Thelma and Louise, or this guy here, how I knew what he meant not by his words, but his eyes, his slight facial tics, and didn't care, I was still that moth who tries to land on a flame.

We went to all the places where the guys who tweaked on speed stayed awake all night. This wasn't the world of Sally and me anymore. It was not warm or soft. There were no songs hummed gently in the background, there was no violin, no massaging the insteps of anyone's feet. They were dangerous places, full of dangerous people, not idyllic, not safe, not harmonious at all, and I felt right at home. These guys could not and would not come down. They stayed up for days, wandering around dark rooms, bumping into each other. They spoke in languages only they understood, conversing in subtle grunts and slight waves of a hand. They possessed open sores, pinpoint pupils, skin taut at the bones, their veins protruding. They shared living spaces—an apartment or a motel room or a cellar underneath a building—or were banging shits with some squaw whose grandmother had a vacant in whatever low-rent building she owned.

I was clean still, dry, really, and the things I wanted—to fuck and kill and be alone—all seemed possible here.

People huddled about couches and coffee tables or disappeared into corners rarely lighted by anything more than the flick of a Zippo or a glowing pipe. I'd be standing alone, feeling quite solitary, and then a gust of breath would warm my face and I'd realize someone had been next to me all along.

This was my first time in L.A., and on subsequent tours, I'd come to know these people more. They lived on ingenuity and guile, never knowing where the next shot was coming from, let alone how they'd stay roofed and fed. They didn't eat so much as subsisted, half a burrito here, a handful of corn nuts there, refilling their roommates' Big Gulps and so forth. They traveled in packs, picking up various hangers-on, none of them with plans beyond now. They'd disappear for weeks, if not years, only to show up suddenly and in nearly the same condition all this time later. They lived in cars and wedged between rocks and under the bridges and windbreaks along Arroyo Seco, collected recyclables and copper, pushed shopping carts all the way down the dusty boulevards until they washed out in Venice or found sustainable barter in the tent towns of San Pedro Street or Slab City, all of them post-hippie, post-grunge and -techno, living on the razor's edge with their nitrous lips and crystal teeth, believing always in the coming end, afraid of everyone.

I always thought Sally possessed an immunity to all this—she was good, different, wholesome, even, but honestly, I have no idea what life was like for her that year. I'd wake up to old coffee and bagels she'd pulled from a dumpster in town. Or a couple bucks. She was thoughtful, romantic. One of her friends had persimmon trees, and they'd bake bread, which she knew I loved, and she'd bring it back to me. We lived an entire fall on this bread. She wanted kids, my kids, wanted to marry me. At one point, I gave her a ring and promised things, and it was my intention we'd be together forever, but life for me has not gone that way. It hasn't gone that way for Sally, either.

Somehow, despite her education, things would soon change for her, and after numerous stops barefoot and halter-topped at one truck stop or another on her way home from music festivals and gatherings and whatnot, Sally eventually became one of these names you'll see written on a slip of paper tacked to a message board outside natural-food stores or on the side of the road between Nyland and Slab City, with a note like "Come home, dear, we miss you" and a phone number.

One evening, I ended up in the cellar but Brian wasn't there, so I went to his room. He cracked his door and stuck his neck out, peering down the hallway before letting me in. A guy was sleeping on the floor who looked a lot like the serial rapist. I whispered to Brian, asking who this guy was, and Brian said just a guy, but his eyelashes fluttered, and I didn't believe him. I'm going to use the bathroom, he said, and turned to leave, but stopped before walking out. He glanced at the guy, then at me. If a thought lingered in his mouth he did not offer it. Just left. And was this code? Was he telling me something? Was it complicity? After he left, I examined his apartment, but other than this guy on the ground, nothing seemed off. It was just one of those sparsely decorated crash pads with very few extras: no couch, no TV, no stereo, no clock, no lamp, no phone. The few clothes Brian owned were piled in a corner. A single mattress—no bedframe—had been pulled up and rested against a wall. Next to a window was a table with an ashtray on top of it, a chair beside it, some burnt tinfoil on the carpeted floor. The guy was still sleeping. I got a closer look. He seemed long enough, lying on the ground. He had that mid-nineties goatee, the sideburns, Caucasian features. I crouched by his head, inspecting his hair. How would the rapist look without a skullcap? It was hard to say.

His eyes opened. They were dark, penetrating, angry.

Violence surged through my body: Had they been right about me? Was I a psychopath?

Who are you? the guy asked.

LATER THAT NIGHT, I did something awful. While Sally tossed and turned and mumbled in her sleep, I stuffed some clothes in my hiking backpack and emptied her socks of all her scholarship money. Then I took a bus downtown, bought a Greyhound ticket, and left. It felt like the worst. I went to Atlanta, saw the people I'd grown up with, all of them toothy, beautiful, and in college now. I was not the kid they remembered. Shame clung to me. I was watery, vague. I smelled bad, looked funny. I have not gone home since.

From Atlanta I went to Tennessee, I think, though maybe that was another time, then Alabama, though that, too, may have been a different year. I'm not sure. My memory of these bus rides all runs together as one long stretch of road and town and the waiting between the two, and why would it not? I knew as long as I kept to the road, I'd be okay. Just keep going, don't stop. That year, you might have found me slouching outside a Walmart, or scratching my balls in front of a rest stop vending machine. I ended up in Baton Rouge, where some of the brothers had moved after leaving the House. They went to meetings, drank Diet Coke, played dominoes, Trivial Pursuit. Bowling was popular entertainment, as was the coffeehouse. For a while, I lounged about their apartments, filling their butt cans and clogging their toilets.

One morning, E-Dog woke me by standing over me and saying my name. Tom, Tommy. Tom motherfucking Macher. Wake up, man, wake up.

I wrapped my sheet tighter. I knew what he'd say. Don't say it, bra, I told him. You don't have to say it.

Seriously, he said. You think it's the meat, but it's not. It never is. It's the protein, bra. How much longer you think you can go on like this?

You think you have to say something, I told him, but you don't.

The difference between you and me right now, he said, is—

I left. Took a train from New Orleans to Beaumont, where there were problems. We got delayed. In San Antonio, we encountered more problems. In El Paso, the tracks doglegged into Juárez, where people lived in cardboard boxes in cardboard towns. I came back to Sally to screw. Afterward, I sat on the bed and stared silently until she looked away. We didn't talk about the money I'd taken. She had class or rehearsal or someone else. When she left, I stole more money from her and hit the road.

I was drinking again, but it wasn't the same. Didn't matter how fucked up I got, nothing changed. I couldn't stop thinking. No matter what. The hole remained. Alcohol didn't work anymore. I couldn't get past the shame of what had come before, not the stealing of Sally's money, not the knowledge that I couldn't hack it at the House, not the understanding of my own futility. Ultimately, the only lesson that had stuck from these places was "That old dumb motherfucker was right." And that is a painful lesson to learn.

I stayed on people's couches or floors, in their beds or basements, in youth hostels, and beneath steps in an alley when it didn't rain. I slept in a car on the mountain or by the water and in eucalyptus groves. I walked around my mom's town, never going to her door unless I knew she was out; I'd stop under eaves and at all-night convenience stores, where I'd smoke and drink hot coffee and watch for cruisers and try to stay out of the rain, always feeling that homeless cold, which is wet and windblown and never—no matter how much coffee you drink—ever going away. I was twenty, maybe. I kept running. Every night was the last, and every morning I said not today.

I'd like to say I thought of other people in all this, but that's not how it works. I'd become a feral thing, pushing against someone else only for warmth. Shit was much, much worse. I called the House, but they didn't have any beds.

Call us in a week, they said.

Instead, I got on another Greyhound bus and headed for Colorado, where, if things didn't improve, I planned to rent a cheap motel room and kill myself.

ELKO HAD WINDOWLESS cinder-block buildings with single neon signs saying "Casino." I spun penny slots one bet after another, didn't care what hit, smoking until my jaw locked and my lungs ached. In the morning, beneath a neon sign, I drank watered-down coffee. Pickups sputtered fumes under a bleak Nevada sky.

At the bus station in Denver, we slept in rotation a few guys at a time while one guy watched for security. We slept on our rucks on the floor or on benches. After a day or so, the guard stopped patrolling and hovered over us, baton snaking from his fist, whacking it against a trash barrel. Now no one slept, and when guys smoked, dude locked them out. It was snowing or about to, cold, and otherwise the same as everywhere else I'd been. I hated myself.

I went to Boulder. It seemed like a good place. I got a cheap motel room. I ate noodles, watched a lot of ESPN, beat off as much as my dick could handle. I was lonely but more so alone. What did it matter what happened to me now? I was anonymous.

Late one afternoon, I stood by a window, watching snow come down and smoking one cigarette after another. After a while, I heard singing. A funeral procession came marching down the street. They chanted, ambling slowly over the dusty white road. Jugglers and fire-breathers, drummers and banjo players. There were firemen and police officers, young girls and old people, lovers and yuppies, the homeless—all with arms linked, their song joyous yet sorrowful. The last of the mourners was a small child. He was not marching at all but instead whirling, arms outstretched, head tilted up, mouth open to the falling snow. With each whirl, he fell another pace behind the rest of the group until he was alone on the empty road, just turning and turning now, not moving, his face sheened over with wet.

Here's what I thought, watching this: Had I done all that had been suggested? Had I fully worked the steps? Had I turned myself over and let go? Was I really going to kill myself without knowing what life was like sober? I still had some money in my pocket. I could give myself another ninety days. I could *always* kill myself.

Fuck it.

Miss A and the Silver Fox

VIC picked me up at the bus station. Vic. What did I tell you? he said. Baseball players . . . .

They don't smoke, Vic, I said.

They don't, he said.

It had the same cracked pavement in its driveway, the same weedy gully in front of it, the same Coke machine, same busted basketball hoop. Different brothers, of course, but the same stories, same stupid shit.

And Program had left. He was gone.

A woman ran it now. Miss A. She liked to talk about dick. It was always dick with her. Dick-dick-dick-dick-dick-dick. And then more dick. I'll say it again, she'd tell us. And then: Don't make me say it again. It didn't matter if we were in group or a one-on-one, in the parking lot, or on the back slab smoking cigarettes.

She described plenty of positions we knew already and many we didn't, such as the butter churner, the thigh master, the triple-reverse-upside-down wheelbarrow, and the snow angel.

If you weren't my client, she'd start off, and I weren't your counselor.

This was bug-eyed shit.

I don't care, she'd say, about your herpes and syphilis, your gonorrhea. HPV don't faze me.

Or she'd get historical about the fucking she used to do behind lonely bars on Airline Highway and in weedy lots next to service stations and cheap motels.

God don't put it where you can reach it, she'd say, if He don't want you playing with it.

Guys thought she was coming on, and when she'd start up with her shit, they'd look the other way, or start finding things to fuck with, like a spot on their shoe or the skin of their palms.

Y'all don't even know, she'd say, what I'm talking about. You haven't even tapped a basic understanding of your own crazy.

The Silver Fox showed up. This was his second time as a social worker here at the House. He was seventy years old, wore a salt-and-pepper perm, a silver handlebar stash, elephant boots, half-buttoned western-styled shirts. Gold chains glittered in his silvery chest hair. He had thirty-two years sober; first third he'd done in Chino. Manslaughter.

He and Miss A hated each other. Openly. Hm, she'd offer, the *Silver Fox,* you say?

And he'd just roll his eyes. *That woman.*

They both refused to call us clients or brothers. Instead we were motherfuckers, junkies, a bunch of roaches, really. But, they could agree, so were they.

He told a story in group once, a straightforward story: For five or six days, he did nothing but slam dope and soil his pants. Same pair of pants. Day after day. This was 1964, maybe '65. San Francisco. Before the hippies came. He drove a drop-top T-Bird, beautiful ride. He could have gone on forever like this, he explained, except he ran out of dope and was idling in an alley when he saw these two cops, these dirty pigs, emerge from a building. They had some bags in their hands. And they began furtively tossing these bags in the dumpster.

He didn't even think about it, he said. Just stepped on the gas, ran those fucks over.

It was a true thing he'd done many years in the Big House, just as it was a true thing Miss A was no virgin. And yet there were inconsistencies: could you really get off a double murder that easy?

There were many conversations, much pooling of our opinions by the basketball hoop.

I didn't care. That's how I knew I'd changed. A difference had come to exist for me in the way I viewed this whole thing: what happened wasn't as important as the truth of a thing.

So what. It didn't matter, this nonsense of Miss A's, and didn't matter if the Silver Fox had imagined his whole creation story while serving a white-collar sentence for hanging bad paper.

It could have happened. It could.

Testimony of Father, Son, and the First of Many

ME and Bob Dirty stopped by the Pizza Buffet to see about this waitress we'd heard many good stories about. There was no way she could disappoint. It was late June and I was still in the House, had about eighty days clean and didn't feel much different about things. Just shitty. Same old, same old, really.

I'll take the lead here, I told Bob Dirty; then you come in with that kielbasa and finish her off.

Oh, and she was pretty, more so than I'd imagined: all curves and gaiety, a real happy-go-lucky type. I worked up a sweat just hearing her polyesters swish between her thighs.

Listen here, I explained, why don't you give me your number before I go and say something to fuck this up.

That's funny, she said. Now, you aren't one of these House boys, are you?

Yup. Both of us.

Nice, she said. Well. Here it is. She scrawled some digits in a curly, looping script. What did you have in mind?

Hand, mouth, or pussy, I said. But anal is fine, too. Honestly, I'd settle for anything.

Don't get me wrong, she said. I would and all. But I don't know you're my thing.

What is your thing? Bob Dirty asked. He was Texas Panhandle all the way, twenty-seven, a con and speedball junkie looking at real time if he didn't finish.

I like boys who go both ways, she said.

Bob Dirty didn't miss a beat, just tossed an arm around my shoulder and pulled me tight, all lispy, limp-wristed, and the like.

Bob's a well-known sausage handler, I told the girl, but she frowned.

We're gay on each other, he informed her. Not that it's anyone's business.

I'll think about it, she told me. But just you, 'kay? I don't trust this other one a bit.

I HAD SOMEWHERE between two and six months left in the House, a long indefinite time, the exactness of it dependent on my behavior, though I didn't think I'd last—ninety days was approaching, and if I wasn't better by then, I promised myself, I'd get a room at the White Rose Motel, drink until I ran out of money, and then hang myself. Bob Dirty, on the other hand, had a few short weeks: his graduation date had been set. While the rest of us played hoops or fuckaround-fuckaround, he'd squat on a parking bump, eyes downcast, interested only in his cigarettes and Zippo. He didn't want to leave. Wasn't anything out there, his eyes would say. Nothing new, anyway, nothing he didn't know.

Maybe the pressure got to him. He began fucking up.

I, too, started prepping for the end. And Jesus, my mom. Who knows what goes on in that woman's mind? She began calling the House, asking for me. I didn't want to take her calls. I didn't want to talk to anyone. I cut off all contact with my family, cut out anyone who'd been in my life to this point. This just made my mom call more. I'd hear the phone ring and start walking. Out to the back slab behind the group room, or into the woods. Brothers tricked me. They'd act like it was their own mom on the phone and then hand the receiver to me.

Sweetie? she'd say.

I didn't know what to tell her now. I mean, what do you tell your mom when you're planning on dying?

Sweetie? Are you there?

I'm sorry, I finally told her. I can't talk to you anymore. Not while I'm here. I'll call you when I get out. Maybe.

I DIDN'T PLAY GAMES, didn't lie or deceive, just signed off the Property to Lutcher, where the Pizza Buffet girl lived, but outside her trailer, sitting on her car's hood, nerves took over and I began speaking of the sky, how queerly green it was above the river and plants, how chemical and lime. She seemed quite bored and then angry and then bored again, and we drove to Pontchartrain, walked its muddy shore where the lake bubbled and frothed and lapped among the reeds. This here, I knew—even before she began popping the various pills she needed to ready herself for what was fixing to happen—was alligator and cottonmouth country, each of these predators silent and creeping and violent and aggressive. Are you ready?

I asked, but her shoulders slumped, her chin dropped, and she began crying.

GUYS FOUND IT FUNNY. They stroked me in Sunday Care and Concern. Bob Dirty and T-Mac, both of them. Going to any lengths. Acting gay for pussy. They had jokes. This guy could not get laid in a . . . Etc. Got a lot of laughs. Miss A listened with a whimsical look, waiting for a point of entry. That's too funny, she said. A real knee-slapper. Little floozy roofies herself and you still couldn't get her done. Shame on you, Tommy. You're pathetic. Tell you what. Fuck up with bitches again—that means anything: talk to them, hang out with them, look at them, anything—you'll be ass out on the road.

This was called No Female Contact and a lot of guys were on it.

What do y'all think? she asked the group. Should we make a pool? I don't give him the end of the month.

It was the twenty-fifth.

Of course, Miss A had a way of making a joke go on forever and, later that week, made me Rec BBG. This afforded me more freedom, an extra hour of curfew, a little more time to myself that I didn't have to explain. Here's some rope, mother-fucker. She laughed. Maybe that extra hour will do you in. My fingers are crossed, she said. I got five bucks riding on this.

Guys uttered condolences. Geez. See you at the White Rose, I guess. It's been okay, they admitted. Not great but decent. Others got more up-front, calling me a fink-fuck, a slick bastard, Mr. Pretend, and so on. I wasn't working a program.

*　　*　　*

THERE ARE ALWAYS decisions we make: Bob Dirty got in a truck and drove to New Orleans, circled back past G-town, and headed west to Lafayette, where he walked the down-town promenade, presumably talking at women. Lafayette is a college town with breweries, dive bars, hip sexy restaurants, boutiques, and yet on its fringes are shanties, cum-dumpster motels, road after road like West with its stores of rock, crystal, Special K, Dilaudid.

I remember when he finally came back, sitting with him on the parking bump and someone asking where he'd gone and what happened, but all he could talk about was crossing the endless Atchafalaya Basin Bridge at sundown, twilight over Whiskey Bay, a stillness in the Spanish moss and on the smooth red water.

There wasn't anything to do now but clear out of his way and hope whoever he dragged down with him wasn't someone you'd miss.

Where were you? Miss A asked in group, but Bob Dirty wouldn't say. Where were you? she asked again, but he sat there, arms crossed, a look of surprise on his face, as if he didn't know where he'd been, not exactly. If you can't say, she said.

I can't.

Tell her about the bridge, someone said. Tell her about the water and the sunlight.

Bob Dirty smiled. He stood up, exited the group room, got in his truck, and left. Not two days later, he found himself in some law scrapes compounding his priors and went to county.

The hard time he faced had doubled, but he made bail. There was nothing for him to do now but keep going. He carried out strong-arm jobs in most of the smaller towns on the west side of the parish and then one day tried to strong-arm a man who wasn't playing and that man shot Bob Dirty in the face and Bob died.

I don't know that I can explain it if you're normal. It's just no, no, no, right until that bottle hits your lips.

I HAD A FEW DOLLARS IN THE BANK, enough for a month or two of heavy use, and I wanted a reward. Rec BBG gave me certain latitudes, and Tyson was fighting Holyfield that weekend. I used Confo money on a pay-per-view box, ordered pizza and wings, bought chips, dip, vanilla and lemon creams, cold drinks. Next I called the Lebanesian, who'd just been released to live down the road in the three-quarter house, which meant he had not graduated yet but was not subject to curfew, Stricts, or Checks. Most important: he had a car.

Pick my ass up, I told him. We're going to Baton Rouge.

Seventeen and severely bipolar, the Lebanesian, when he was still at the House, spent many days catatonic on the couch or floor. Prone, eyes dead, he'd finger the shag fibers as if they were new and strange. I wanted to be there for him and would tell him I loved him and offer to listen if he wanted to share, but he'd just keep up with those dead eyes, touching the polyester. Do you want to be alone? I'd ask, and if he didn't answer, I'd turn to go, but he'd grab at my ankle and pull it to his cheek, all curled and fetal and quivering. Or he'd lie between my bed and Captain Ron's, the Captain snoring, talking me to sleep. I'd wake hours later and he'd still be prattling on, never about anything. Then he'd go way up, gorge himself on all-you-can-eat buffets, hot white buns, Doritos. His weight fluctuated between fat and extremely obese. Once I saw him run up the hood and over the roof and trunk of a car. Whose car is that? I asked, thinking it was a joke. Don't know, he said. Who cares? He'd hop on a table and gyrate like Elvis during Dinner Group. He was unstoppable, a true sick fuck, criminally intelligent, probably best served somewhere else—what do Stricts matter when you can't get it together?

I was standing outside a meeting with Roger M., who sponsored a lot of brothers, and Nob, when the Lebanesian pulled into the parking lot doing about five miles an hour. Roger M., who was certifiable, told us, Watch this, and walked into the driveway and stood in front of the car. He was being funny, I think. He held his hand up as if he were a traffic cop. Annoyance flashed in the Lebanesian's eyes. Anyone could've read his lips: What the fuck are you doing? Get out of the way, dude. Move!

But Roger M. didn't move and the Lebanesian plowed him over, crumpling the old man at his fender and discarding him on the pavement.

It should've signaled a shift to the surreal; my testimony would change; the night would grow dreamlike, full of possibility and dead ends. I asked Nob if that really happened and he said yes and indeed Roger M. was on the pavement collecting his Big Book and glasses. But here's the thing about the surreal: I simply stepped over Roger M. and got in the car, slathered my neck and package with some of the Lebanesian's cologne, and we reversed out of the parking lot, business as usual.

*   *   *

WE WENT TO what would become the usual—Perks, Coffee Call, at each place approaching girls if we saw them. It didn't matter if she had a guy with her already. We didn't care. We can go outside if you want, we'd say, or you can sit dick in hand while I state my case. Do you live at home? Have a car? Are you in school? Of legal age? What're your finances like? At Highland Grounds, a sexy redhead sat reading *Catch-22*. She greeted me warmly, setting her book down as if she'd been waiting for me. I knew she was the one. Where do you live? she asked. When I told her the name of the town, she shrieked in delight. Oh my God. She was from there, too. And oh, man. I bet you live in the House, she said. House boys are hot as fuck. She couldn't help it. She liked bad boys and I seemed bad, real bad. Will you cum on my pillow, she asked, and then take all my money?

I might even steal your car, I said, winking at the Lebanesian. This was easier than finger-banging a Holstein.

She traced the inseams on my jeans, fingers crept uptown, disengaged, all fuck-eye and smiles. She wanted to work on trains, maybe be a train stewardess, whatever they're called, or a conductor. Free travel, she said, I'm practically a gypsy, a real-life hippie and poet.

Gosh, I said. How interesting. What does someone like you do for work, anyway?

I'm a dancer, she said.

What kind? I asked. Modern? Jazz? Ballet?

The Lebanesian shoved me aside. What *club*?

Southern Kumfort, she said, touching my collar and buttons,

grabbing hold of my shirt, twisting its fabric in her fingers. I'm headed to my friend's for a fitting if you want to come.

We were so close I tasted her mouth. This breath of hers, wow. It warped my brain, turned my dick to stone. But the Lebanesian pushed in close as well. The three of us were nuzzling one another, almost. I looked into her eyes and my blood surged and then I saw his dull pharmaceutical stare and my blood waned.

Do you mind? I asked the Lebanesian.

Huh?

You know. Can you, like, fuck off for an hour or something? Is that—is it—am I asking too much?

He was none too pleased. I see how it is. I can't even watch, huh?

Pick me up at eleven-thirty. Is that enough time? I asked the girl. Curfew was twelve-thirty.

Sure, she said. Whatever you need.

Dang. All I needed was thirty seconds. Mostly just to fidget with the condom. I was fixing to screw! Push out, I told the Lebanesian. I'm going to convince her to fall in love with me. We're going places. Maybe Alaska or some other frontier. I'd settle for Pierre Port at this point, even Central. I don't care.

Some are sicker than others, he said. I guess.

Just meet me at Louie's Diner at eleven-thirty.

SHE PRANCED ABOUT in pasties and a G-string, tossing down Nembutals. On a coffee table was a handle of Old No. 7, a gram of cocaine.

Go on. She waved her hand. Help yourself.

But I didn't need that stuff to love.

225

Please, she cooed, climbing on top of me, grinding my junk. Not even *just one?* She held a glass of wine to my lips. One line, a pill? If you drink this, she offered, you can fuck me in the asshole or *whatever.*

No, no, I said, no, no, no, no, no, no, no, *well*—turn around, I guess; better see this thing, at least.

She turned, bent, spread her cheeks, red-eye in my face. Wow, *okay!*

I stuffed my thumb inside, but she wiggled free. Not yet! Hold on! She had some Astroglide in her purse. NASA uses this, she said. In space. Go ahead, smear it all over your body if you want. Now, are we fixing to party or *what?*

My mind tumbled in a low heat and gentle cycle: Yes, no, yes, no, yes, no. Let me explain what'll happen if I have just one.

We'll fuck like mallards, she said.

Mallards rape, I said.

I know that, she told me. You think I don't know *that?* I'm into *that.*

One equals two equals three, I said, and then I'll be fucked up a long, long time.

I have until Tuesday, she said. That's when I work. That long enough?

What about Alaska? What about the old Al-Can?

Have a drink, she said. Relax.

Oh, God. It was eleven-thirty. Hold on, I told her. Be right back.

I WALKED TO LOUIE'S, but the Lebanesian's car wasn't in the parking lot, so I went inside and looked in the bathroom and kitchen. I asked a waitress, but she hadn't seen anyone that looked like him. I walked up Perkins, peeked in the Varsity, asked the door guy, the coat-check girl. I walked down Chimes to Highland Grounds, the Library Bar—I looked everywhere. I walked back to Louie's and waited. Then I asked that same waitress, but she just shook her head. I'm sorry, she said. I sat a long while outside Louie's. It was well past midnight. I'd missed curfew. I began feeling sorry for myself. He'd left me. Like my dad and brothers, like when my mom kicked me out. I made a decision. I needed to stock up. I wanted enough booze to ride out whatever was fixing to happen, comfortably. Maybe four days' or a week's worth. I had twenty bucks and an all-or-nothing feeling, like when you're hungry and someone offers you a cookie but you don't want a cookie. You want the whole motherfucking bag. Across from Louie's was a strip mall with an ATM. At one point, the strip mall had a grocery store, a record shop, and a Thai restaurant, but only the ATM and a bar called Chelsea's remained. Everything else had been boarded and abandoned long ago. It was on the edge of campus where the blocks turned rough, and I thought some about the promise of a rough turn and roads like West. Maybe I'd keep wandering or wander this way later or wander come Tuesday when she had work. I didn't care anymore. It was over for me.

I slid my card in the ATM, punched my code, and waited. I waited a long-ass time. The machine spat my card out. A message flashed on the ATM's screen: insufficient funds. I put my card in and tried a smaller number, but the same thing happened again and so I put my card in again and tried once more, but the message kept appearing until it dawned on me. My account wasn't the problem. It was the machine. It was empty.

ALLOW ME A DIGRESSION.

Captain Ron came from Panama via Ohio. He had 20/10 vision, blue eyes, a squat, confident build and square jaw, wavy blond hair. His family was all political, power brokers, governors, presidents, as far back as you could trace it, but his mother was merely a mistress, and it had long ago been explained to the Captain that he would never match up. He had wanted to be an air force pilot, and his attributes would have served the corps well. Athletic, driven, he held black belts in most mainstream martial arts. He wore sandals, colorful shirts, and torn jean shorts—what people used to call Daisy Dukes, ball or butt huggers—cut so high that Miss A used to keep him away from her children. From a standstill, he'd leap and kick our hands.

He worked at the Piggly Wiggly. He owned a collection of guayaberas in every color, every pastel, every guava, avocado, lilac, and strawberry, a collection so extensive that he gave brothers as many as we wanted, one two three four five shirts. He owned a ten-speed bike, a stereo—one of the last premium towers made—thousands of CDs. He owned an espresso maker.

He slept in the bed next to me most of that spring and early summer, him window, me wall, and we talked about our fathers, comparing his four visits with my own four or five encounters, or we held forth on what it had been like *out there* sleeping in cars smelling of mildew and rot whose floorboards had rusted through and whose windows didn't work. He told me about

Ohio, the gone factories and wheat, endless roads and country-side. We talked about being the bastard kids of known families, what it had been like to have an exotic last name in the land of football. I met his mother, a blonde turned ash gray, her once-flirtatious face turned stern, lips thin, high cheekbones and skin soft as an eighteen-year-old's. He stocked our fridge with bulk-purchase pies, sold them a dollar or two a slice, a four-to-one markup, and poured espresso as a loss leader.

Intense, obsessed, neurotic, but also laid-back, relaxed: if you broke a rule in front of the Captain, he might wave a mockingly comical finger, but there'd be no group called, no record of your infraction. He was a don't-worry-about-it brother, a just-forget-it type. He did not call people bitch, moth-erfucker, junkie, sicko, or any of our common nomenclature. You couldn't drop a "bra" when addressing him directly. He wouldn't have it. My friend, he'd say, I am no female under-garment. He was jocular, glib, and yet his clowning was all epidermis—he remained firmly rooted in a false vision from his past and knew it. He was twenty-six years old, and the longer he stayed sober, the more he had to face an awful truth: he wasn't going to be a pilot, he wasn't going to be a diplomat, he wouldn't be in the Secret Service, even, and would never hold any kind of government office. And in those unspoken moments, after the laughter between us died, after the argu-ments over how high we might turn the AC waned, when the rains came, as they came most nights that spring, and we were quiet, I could hear in his tossing and turning all those familiar worries—the what now and how will I amount to.

We giggled about his outfits, made fun of his jocular demeanor or the sheer number of possessions he'd brought with him, all of which he met with a dignified and blasé wave of his hand—it was over-the-top, junkie, but so what? He enjoyed music. He liked riding his bike. Who doesn't want to wear a different guayabera every day of the month? Have a slice of pie, he'd say. Here's a chocolate cream, on the house. Would you like an espresso?

He knew how this thing went: if you wanted sympathy, you were stupid; if you thought someone would yes-man you, you were insane; bitching, moaning, and whining were all met with shrieks—poor me! poor me! pour me another drink! A popular expression was: Don't strangle yourself patting your own back. Put another way: what happened to us has not been pretty. We have OD'd or jumped out windows, off roofs. We have died from self-inflicted gunshot wounds, severed our heads with shotgun blasts, our hearts have exploded from self-imbibed hotshots, we've been riddled with holes on home invasions gone wrong, hanged ourselves in cellars, barns, from shower nozzles, and in strangers' garages. Captain Ron, within a few months of this event, drove his motorcycle up Highway 30 to a four-way intersection where many eighteen-wheelers blew by on their way to the interstate. Each time a truck passed, he gunned his bike across the highway, narrowly avoiding getting hit until he finally timed it just right and was run over. No one viewed it as anything other than suicide. He is one of many. And long before he bought the bike, he knew he was done living. I knew it, too. We all knew it about him. But what could we say? What do you tell the condemned? Do you offer nothing but compassion and kindness? I wonder about it. Where does kind stop being kind, and with whom? How can I offer grace when often my grace only leads to further pain? When do you offer the pillow? When do you take that same pillow and wrap it around eyes and ears?

NO ONE WAS WITH ME at the ATM, so no one can say if it's true that the machine lacked money. I didn't drink. And I didn't get laid. At some point, I found myself hurtling along Main, through downtown, past St. Theresa's, the Western Auto, and the kidney bean cannery, at eighty-five miles an hour while the stripper alternated bumps of cocaine and Nembutal. She drove the kind of car you might expect a junkie gypsy to drive, and nothing on it worked. She dropped me off either near the House or where the Lebanesian lived: it didn't matter to me where she dropped me off. I knew I wasn't going home. I vaguely remember running through someone's yard and a field and some woods and crouching around in the bushes. I planned, and had been planning for the last two hours, to break in through a window and strangle the Lebanesian while he slept. His face had become the face of all my failings and shame. By leaving me in Baton Rouge, he'd cost me the House. It wasn't my behavior. But his. Of course, it is one thing, I understand, to murder someone out of anger or momentary lapse, you are jealous, you are enraged, something snaps, and your mind grows blank, but quite another to hold a murderous feeling for hours on end. By the time I found an unlocked window, I'd stopped thinking altogether. I pulled myself into his home and quietly entered his bedroom. But he wasn't in bed. I tried the bathroom, dining room, kitchen, and living room, but found only Bill, half-asleep on the couch watching highlights from Vegas. Uncle Bill had been around a long time by now, so long he seemed much, much older than his nineteen years. He'd been Kitchen BBG when I got in the House, but was now just a guy who stocked shelves at Walmart. He was not surprised to see me. The Lebanesian's at the House, he informed me, and then fell asleep. Uncle Bill was going to die soon. He was probably already using.

From the moment I woke Captain Ron, he began talking me down. Don't worry about it. Say you forgot to sign in. No one's looking at those logs. I'll tear the log out. We'll forge them. Seriously.

What about the Lebanesian? I asked.

Can't be mad at crazy, he said.

I'ma kill that fucker.

No, no. How about this? I'll get up. Sign you in myself. Meanwhile, have some pie. Have an espresso. I have decaf.

I don't want to get you in trouble, I said, though in fact, by telling him, I already had.

He grinned at my shirt—an apricot long-sleeved guayabera. You old devil, he said. Get any? Good for you.

Ron.

Nobody's going to know, Tommy; just walk on down there, sign in for twelve-thirty. You forgot. It happens. We all forget sometimes.

I HAD A FEW Negative Contracts now, though none seemed truly dangerous. At worst, it was all caught head, banged ass— pseudo-normal sexual shit filed under hard to avoid—nothing serious. No one was shooting dope in the group room john or smoking crack behind the dumpster. The pay phone had been removed; neither strawberries nor their pimps loitered in the parking lot. It was a different House, I had different goals. If you told me shit, I was ratting your ass out, more than likely, if it affected me.

And yet consider the first of many Hair-pie incidents: I'd gone inside my apartment one afternoon to shower and clean up for a meeting when I heard or felt an excitement bristling in the air. Perhaps it was just the whisking of a satin shirt against skin, a rustling of cotton, a shuffling of flesh. It was half-heard. I didn't want to know. If Staff or some confrontational type had come busting through the door for Checks, we'd be fucked, whoever was in that back bedroom for doing whatever they were doing, and me via proxy. I was sure it was sexual, could tell by the air, how thick it felt, how paused. Sexual relations on Property were strictly prohibited, more so even than using, a bootable on-the-spot offense. The back bedroom door was cracked open. A dresser had been moved in front of it, blocking the view. This was too shady to ignore. The dresser alone gave me an NC if I didn't report it. I figured I'd push the dresser back, shut the door, that's all: I didn't want to be involved, just wanted the scenario to unfold privately. But I accidentally looked up. Hair-pie was sitting on the back bed next to another brother. They sat close, like two lovers examining a photo album. This other brother was a young man of maybe seventeen who didn't think he had a problem. I don't remember his name. He was leaving soon, I forget why. Maybe his insurance had lapsed or his parents were calling him back or his ambivalence about recovery had gone too far and Staff had given him the boot. Anyway, he was leaving. And these two, in their own way, were saying goodbye. SOP demanded I confront and call group, get everything in the open, process, deal with, weed the bad seeds. We are part and parcel, we were taught, to what we ignore. But here's the deal: I wanted to be liked. I didn't want Hair-pie to get kicked out. I know I'm not responsible for anyone else's actions, and yet I know, too, that if it weren't for the brave honesty of many, I wouldn't be here. It could be such a weird thing sometimes, the fine line that blurs right and wrong in this brotherhood of fucked-up men, where we'll walk so far down a road with someone else, holding their hand, only to turn back when our stomach begins to twist up. At that age, stripped of everything, what else is there but unquestioned sexuality? Fighting your own thinking matters, fighting loneliness. We loved each other, and in that love, broad things emerged. I told myself I didn't know what was going on between them, though before I looked up, I knew already.

I shut the door and walked away.

I regret this.

THERE WAS A MOMENT ON MAIN when the stripper nodded out at the wheel and the car lurched onto the curb. We rolled on the curb for a block until a parking meter knocked a mirror off. Sparks shot from the undercarriage. She came to, did a bump, and asked me through watering eyes if I wanted to die. I didn't. I knew that then. *Not yet.* I'd made a huge mistake.

The House wasn't much. The food was awful, beds small, ceilings low, rugs old, blankets institutionally thin. It was, in other words, poor, sad, forlorn, decrepit, a strip of weathered apartments on a run-down road, a place people went before they died. But it's what I thought of when she asked me if I wanted to die. The basketball hoop, the dumpster next to the group room. Had the porch railing already come down?

I wandered down the front porch to sign in, a bootable offense, a huge NC between me and the Captain, peeking in living room windows. Halfway to the group room, I stopped. All of BBG had gathered about the TV in Room Four. Nob was bent over himself on the couch, tying a bootstrap. Hymen lay supine on the floor, arms and legs splayed, chin to the side. He was laughing about something. Through the window, he seemed tired yet happy. Pope on a Rope reclined in an easy chair, strumming a guitar. Hair-pie was in the kitchen, down-stroking in its corner. And in the middle of them all, holding court and enjoying a slice of cold pizza, was none other than the Lebanesian. He looked up at me. Did he catch my eye? Was that surprise on his face? Did he know?

I kicked open the door and made straight for him, but Nob jumped between us. Hymen involved himself. Hymen was a big man, and though I'm tall, I'm not big like him. Thick as an oak and every bit firm, he picked me up and set me on the couch, sat down beside me, one arm half loving and half restraining around my shoulder, the other arm holding me by the chest.

Easy, T-Mac, Nob said. Why you sweating?

The Lebanesian's eyes moved left-right, right-left, telling me shut up, do not speak, just sign the Negative Contract.

Tell them, I said.

No.

IT SOUNDS LIKE RHETORIC, bullshit, a con, but I owe those guys my life. I owe the Lebanesian my life. I owe the stripper my life. I owe Captain Ron my life. I owe those brothers in Room Four my life. I am lucky.

Nob, who'd never wanted anything more than to be liked, called group. I don't know why. Perhaps it was just a knee-jerk thing, a reaction outside himself that led to the brave and extraordinary, or maybe he'd finally seen enough and knew where he didn't want to end up. In group, it all came out. Brothers were pissed. They called me a Jack Rehab bitch. Wait, Chicago Pete said, you didn't drink *or* fuck and you're waking me up to talk about it. Fuck you, pussy! Dude walked out. Vic said Miss A would come in the morning and boot my ass. For now, I should sleep, but I didn't sleep and instead sat out behind the group room with Nob, Hymen, Hair-pie, and the Lebanesian. Around five a.m., some House alumni passed by on their way to a meeting, did I want to go? Sure, I said. At the meeting, they pointed me toward a man who'd become my sponsor, and from the first time we spoke, I knew that no matter what happened at the House, if Miss A kicked me out or not, I'd be safe, I didn't have to drink again. It is a weird thing, feeling spiritual about something. Tell me all you want about randomness, the lack of explanation, there is no God. I get it. God doesn't care if I bang the stripper or drink, and yet I survived through no will of my own.

Miss A moved Captain Ron out of my room and moved Nob in. Then she put me on Scribes. My only contact in the House was Nob, but I didn't want to talk to Nob, and he didn't want to talk to me. The term of my Scribes was indefinite. I would sit in the corner and write about how pussy was just an extension of my alcoholism until I either ran away again or learned something. I sat in that corner nine days. Nine. Two decades later, I am still writing about that extension.

The Lebanesian drank again. So did Chicago Pete, but I hear both are alive now. Captain Ron killed himself. Pope on a Rope disappeared. After a few weeks, Nob and I began speaking, and once we started speaking, we couldn't stop. Him, me, Hymen, Morning Wood, and Hair-pie stayed up many nights on the back slab, telling each other the shit of ourselves. Later, I was released to the three-quarter house, where the Lebanesian and Uncle Bill had lived. Nob moved, too. So did Hair-pie. Then Hymen and Morning Wood. For a while, we circulated back to group every Sunday, Tuesday, and Thursday, and though our Tasks still applied and our actions were still monitored, such as I remained on No Female Contact, none of the other drudgery concerned us now. We weren't subject to Hours or Areas, didn't have to wake up at any specific time. We could watch TV at noon, if we wanted, or stay out all night.

These men had become my family, but our work had just begun.

The Trailer Crew,
as Explained at a Dinner Party

AFTER being released, the five of us rented a pair of trailers in a small trailer court among a stand of pines on a dead-end road off Highway 934 off Highway 431, not far from Diversion Canal and Bayou Terrace in the floodplains of the Amite and Lake Maurepas between French Settlement and Acy in a Louisiana backwater thirty miles from Baton Rouge. This was a no-place town. Its post office was inside a DIY home-improvement store. A small strip mall with a nail salon, a grocery, and a few gas pumps completed its lonely business loop. On the 934 were beef cattle and horse farms, modular homes and prefabs, eroding ranches, cypress barns peeled back by weather, soy and strawberry and oil fields. The House was a twenty-minute drive through swampy softwood forests. It was, in other words, a place we could've disappeared in, though we aimed to live here same as we lived in the House, with accountability and an earnest desire to better ourselves. We practiced showing up, being present, trusting in God's will. We were doing it. And aimed to keep doing it, no matter what.

Me, Hair-pie, and Nob lived in one trailer; Morning Wood and Hymen rented the ten-wide next door. The four of them worked in the call center for a medical company, and I had graduated from janitor to cleaning crew to swinging a hammer at a local construction company. The job took me all over the surrounding parishes—I framed condos at Pelican Point, hung drywall along the river, or formed slabs in Geismar— and paid six and a half dollars an hour, cash, which was a quarter more than the call center, ten extra bones a week, forty a month, and though I needed the money, more so I was proud of the job. I liked working outdoors and dealing with the weather, took pride in my tan and thickening fore-arms. Most days I wore only shorts and a pair of sneakers to work—no drawers or shirt, no socks. And I was learning a trade, something I'd always be able to hold on to. This was what I'd do, who I'd be.

We were all twenty, twenty-one, twenty-two, all sober a year and intent on staying that way. Except Hair-pie, who was *Hair-pie,* we were all highly male—masturbatory, loud, loose with advice, cynicism, and hope. We admired those with "good sobri-ety": what meetings you attended was important, who sponsored you, what parts of the Big Book you read and quoted, who you ran with, what you said, and did you stay late at those meetings or leave early. We made five to seven meetings a week, were sponsored by respected members of the community, actively participated in alumni group at the House, sponsoring young brothers, driving dudes to the doctor and airport, had the keys to our home group and made coffee, set up literature, cleaned coffee urns, stacked chairs, swept, and mopped. We attended A.A. conventions, sober dances, and crawfish boils. We worked the steps. And yet we were young. We practiced laughter; sac-tapping and wrestling were common. We perpetrated prank phone calls, petty vandalism, bought pellet guns, would shoot out the windows of each other's trailer, always straddling that cusp of going too far, the line between youth and responsibility. We watched a shit-ton of porn, ate shit food—TV dinners and Van Camp's—drank coffee, DC, Sunny Delight. And we drove around a lot. To the supermarket, Sonic, or Mickey D's, where girls needed ogling. We had our rounds.

Still, we had limits, set boundaries, and agreed: no sex until we made eighteen months.

As for Hair-pie, well, he was an enigma—I'll say *different.* He was good-looking, rich, yet almost too much so; his looks came off as dishonest, somehow, untrustworthy. When he was embarrassed, his cheeks flushed a mellow rose. He had soft, easily irritated skin, hairless arms, a smooth forehead—I think he plucked his eyebrows. He wore chinos, pressed collared shirts, conservative leather belts, boat shoes or wing tips, argyle socks, nothing cool. He didn't smoke or drink coffee, not drip, anyway, but lattes, cappuccinos, *herbal tea.* He liked food, but not what we ate, and instead nibbled on crisps, pancetta, funky-smelling cheese, sugar cookies, raw fish, well-marbled beef. He read Wordsworth and Yeats, listened to Bach and Beethoven, wore a silk robe, cleaned his glasses with a specific silk cloth, made his bed every morning, practiced oral hygiene, general cleanliness, never smelling of BO, swamp-ass, fromunda cheese, or any of these other things. He never had a hangnail and never just made up his hair but combed it first and then brushed it, rolling his part over and over until it stuck true, firm and lasting, whereupon he patted it with proteins, amino acids, egg whites, cholesterol, and sea salt.

Rumors regarding his sexuality swirled.

Of course, I'd seen that thing once, that NC back in the House, but had filed this information away in that complacent part of my mind, where I leave things be.

Other stories emerged. Beating off was a popular activity in the trailers. Our stockpile of porn was apocalypse-ready. We had boxes and boxes of it, but only one couch and one TV. Next to the couch, our front door offered a head-high diamond-shaped window where we could look out at a visitor and a visitor could look in at us. I say all this because standard practice called for us to return home and, one by one, take our seat on this couch and unwind. Late one afternoon Nob was watching a film from the series *The Best of Caught from Behind,* Kleenex next to him, stiffy out, when he felt a gentle wind, as if a ghost were in the room, what you might call a sort of "third hand." It was almost sundown, dark outside under the pines, and Nob told himself, Fuck it, no one's home. He fast-forwarded through some fellatio to the hard-core banging, but his face flushed, his dick grew limp: he couldn't shake the feeling of someone else. He got up. The front door's window was fogged over, and he yanked it open. Here was Hair-pie, glassy-eyed, breathing heavy, his britches tented.

Word spread. It got so we couldn't even tell a story from the trailers without offering Hair-pie downstroking in the corner as a show of veracity. No one would believe us.

I SAY ALL THIS because I am forty now, and clean. I have long-term sobriety. I've been clean way, way longer than I ever used. This is mostly a chemical absence. I'm prone to the same shortcomings, as always. But it's misleading to say we stay fully submerged under the rock of addiction, a leper can't change their spots, etc. I'm not who I once was. If you want proof of psychic change, I'd point to my cash-register honesty and lack of thievery, etc., yet as much as I claim this, further inventory proves otherwise: just last week, in a pinch, I pocketed a roll of toilet paper from a local institution. I didn't want to use their crapper, is how I justified it. But I'm not replacing that roll. I'm not mailing them a check for a dollar sixty-nine, whatever. I don't lie awake regretting it. I say this because I'm not always aware of my own intentions. I have a mistrust of me. At core, I'm selfish, single-minded, obsessed, and while I no longer steal with a capital S or deal or hustle or search for hideaway keys under doormats or flowerpots, the thinking remains: I will springboard off you. I don't think twice about the toilet paper or what I got to do to nut. I'm clean, but a user still. Sugar makes me feel good, TV takes my mind off shit, strange pussy cures depression. I can get so anxious and unremitting that I don't clean my house, don't eat, don't pay bills, and shut myself off from friends, family, loved ones. If you say there's copper in that vacant, I start thinking about who I know with a truck and where to find a pry bar. I exhibit behavior, in other words, am prone to usury, and all the blanket statements about who I am based on where I've been still have some basis of truth.

But I'm also educated now; I possess what's called a terminal degree; I've taught at a Big Ten university. People trust me. I housesit from time to time, even babysit. And I get invited places—galas, art openings, lunch with boards of trustees, artists' residencies, dinner parties. And it was at one of these events, with everyone dressed appropriately, the napkins folded correctly, and the wine poured exact, after four courses of local greens and grass-fed meat, when I got bored. My boredom is rarely a good thing. I started telling some of the trailer crew stories.

THE FIRST ONE IS ALWAYS THIS: Hair-pie came back from a visit to his mom's offering only a left-handed shake. We were big on handshakes in those days, big on hugs, big on confrontation. No one trusted a left-handed shake. What the fuck is wrong with you? Nob asked, but Hair-pie shoved his right hand into his pocket and began whistling as if nothing had been said. Hey, Nob said, show me your hand.

Hair-pie held up his left hand.

No, Nob said. The other one.

Hair-pie began looking about our living room for somewhere to hide. I'm busy, he explained, and marched into the kitchen and scrubbed his hand under the faucet. Wood got involved. Then Hymen. They wanted to know what the hell he was doing.

Hair-pie slipped free and had almost made it to his car when Hymen reached out and horse-collared him to the ground, ripping his hand from his pocket.

It was orange. Bright orange. His palms, fingers. All of it orange. He held his wrist now, looking at his orange hand as if trying to find the right words.

I couldn't find any lube, he said. Had to use some dumb cream called All-Over-Me-Gold.

No one was mad now. Does this mean your cock is orange, too?

I was at my mom's, he sobbed. It's all she had.

*　　*　　*

WE BULLIED HIM, I told the people at this party. And then, feeling that deep burning shame that reddens my ears and swells my throat, my voice muted: We were young.

I didn't go into details. Didn't mention his hairy chest, how we used to hold him down, pull his shirt up, and rub a tennis racket over him until his chest hairs tangled in the webbing. I did not mention the time I punched him so hard in the throat that for a little while we thought he might die. Somehow, despite my naïveté, I knew better.

We used duct tape to bind his wrists. We'd hold him, one of us grabbing his bound wrists, one on each of his ankles, the fourth beating him about his torso and back. We poked our index fingers into his sternum or forehead until his eyeballs turned red and watered, thick with blood.

Nope. Couldn't say any of that. *We bullied him.* I could feel my throat thicken, my voice failing me.

After I slugged him in the throat, his rosy cheeks paled. He dropped to one knee and then his belly, kicking his legs spastically as if a bucking donkey. He made noises, gurgles and gasps—it sounded like he was choking, maybe on his own tongue.

I provided little backstory, bare exposition—the pertinent details of knowing each other from a halfway house seemed good enough. I merely said, After the House, five of us lived in the backwater, in the floodplains, talked about how high the water got in our yards in the spring, when walking between our trailers felt like sloshing through a creek.

*　　*　　*

THAT CHRISTMAS WE BOUGHT Nob a Pocket Pal, which is a plastic sleeve fashioned to look like a vagina. It had a small tuft of faux pubic hair, garish faux labia, a slot to add lube. One online review describes it as "very close to the real thing, except it wears out after a while." It was funny, a gag, but also useful. Nob liked it. And it liked Nob. But Nob was going away—home, I think, for the holidays—and left it behind. While he was gone, I decided to steal it, hide it in Hair-pie's room, make him out as a sicko. I admit I'm dumb. I went into Nob's room and looked under his bed and in his dresser and closet. Then I thought about things. I wasn't framing a careful man. Hair-pie behaved desperately; I needed to act desperately, too. I ripped Nob's mattress off the bed, flipped it against the wall, broke whatever dishware had collected on the nightstand, emptied his drawers, got after his shoe boxes full of CDs and old pictures, smashed a lamp, rifled his papers. Afterward, I rocked on my haunches and collected my breath. The Pocket Pal was already gone.

Nob wasn't happy when he returned. He screamed and screamed. What happened to my damn room? What happened to my stuff?

I couldn't be bothered to get off the couch. I knew what had happened to his stuff.

He went to Hymen and Wood's trailer and screamed at them and came home and screamed at me. Hymen and Wood appeared. Then G-Dub. Even Three Dog stopped by.

Macher, Nob demanded. What the hell. Tell me: what happened to my stuff?

I can't even begin to guess, I said.

Come look at my room, he pleaded. You got to see it.

I don't want to, I said. It'll just make me angry.

But others were poking about now, so, not to seem suspicious, I did, too. Torn, shredded, broken: nothing surprised me about any of it. I felt small, red in the ears.

Nob continued to stomp about, thinking about things. Finally, he banged on and then pulled at Hair-pie's door, but it was locked. The rest of us got involved. We were forceful.

Hair-pie opened the door with the kind of desperation on his face that a man will get just before he knowingly beats off with tanning cream.

We shoved past him and into his small room and began tossing it same as I'd tossed Nob's, ripping his blankets and sheets off, pulling pillows from his pillowcases, shoving his bookcase over, picking up his books and slamming them on the ground. He had potted plants, hanging plants, vased plants, all of which we turned upside down and shook, emptying flora and soil on the carpet. We whacked his shoes against each other as if ridding them of sand. We wound his towels and silk robes into whips, unfurled them on one another. Guys got hold of his chonies, lifted him from the ground. We pinched at his nipples, flicked his nuts one ball at a time, tore at receipts and ledgers, manuals and instruction books, ripped pages from volumes of poetry, and took up his many geodes and banged them until their crystals smoothed. He had horded packages of snack foods—Ding Dongs, Nutter Butters, and Cool Ranch Doritos; we devoured them all. At some point, Morning Wood emerged from the bathroom, his face covered in toothpaste and shaving cream, the Pocket Pal in his hand.

Look what I found, he said. Fresh used!

*   *   *

THE TRUTH IS, we had fun together, but often words. Hymen used to beat the shit out of me every afternoon. We'd get to swinging on each other and he'd end up on top, pin my arms down with his knees. He'd take my face and rub it into the shag until I bled. Eventually, he set me on fire one afternoon and I almost burned alive, but that's not this story.

Their trailer was a ten-wide, ours a twelve. Both were seventy feet long. When we weren't wrestling or shooting at one another, we'd gather rocks, build a fire pit, grill brats and marshmallows. We worked the steps. After I punched Hairpie, I made amends, and after Hymen set me on fire, he made amends. Both amends were public affairs, with witness, feeling, and love. We were truly sorry. And truly loved each other. We were going to stay sober forever, together. That was our plan.

People laughed at us. And mocked us. But also, they admired us. What we had out there was coveted. While other brothers from the House marched out to the crack houses and bars of southeastern Louisiana to disappear and die, we stayed sober. Soon enough, a clump of young girls from a local woman's treatment center started appearing at the meetings we attended. They'd wait for us in the darkened hallways of churches and health clinics. There wasn't much to say. It was only a matter of time. They started calling our trailers, their number sadly lighting our caller ID. They never actually spoke, just breathed a lot. Then there'd come hoarse, quickened laughter and a dial tone.

AS MUCH AS I LIKE to claim perspective, this whole streetwise knockaround thing, and as much as I *have* been around and seen shit in my day, I am an absolute greenhorn when it comes to the dinner or wine-and-cheese party, the glad-handing, the lunch with your board of trustees. I just ain't that sophisticated. This scene is above and beyond me. I'm a rube. I don't know what things to omit, have no clue what not to say, and most important—can't stop myself. I know, as I'm joking about these dumb things—the shits and giggles and fuckaround-fuckaround—I'm not telling *the story*, and instead just giving culture, background, exposition for something darker. I don't want to continue. That's the thing. I don't want to tell the story. But I have to. Because it is there now, heavy on my chest, the memory of it.

The morning after the dinner party, I called Wood. It'd been thirteen years since I saw him, and by now we only spoke when someone died. I could hear a silent question linger after he said my name: Who?

I was at a—I could barely say it—dinner party last night, I told him.

Uh-huh, he said.

Started telling some of the trailer crew stories.

No doubt. Get the Cockwork Orange in?

Yup.

Pocket Pal?

Yeah, that, too.

This was in Provincetown, where I was in residence for seven months at the Fine Arts Work Center, and I was standing in the parking lot of a resort that had been boarded up for the season. In front of me was a pier with boatlifts. Gray seals rolled in the water. I heard Wood's breathing change. A Zippo clicked, tobacco crackled in a flame. He inhaled deeply, then exhaled.

Anything else?

Yes, I said, expecting he'd laugh over how stupid I am, but he didn't.

Well, he said.

And he was right. *Well.* That one word said it all.

HER NAME WAS TAMMY Z. and she had a reputation. Burt had banged her and so had Dorn, but a lot of guys had. We knew she'd been double-teamed at a frat party and banged over the hotline by the GM at Olive Garden, where she worked, and by the bartender in dry storage and a busboy on the loading dock—even the dishwasher got his turn one Tuesday afternoon. She'd been banged by Alabama Bill outside the Step Study and by Recidivist Pete at the library. She'd been banged in her car and in strangers' cars and in more than a dozen apartment complexes and on the side of the road and on top of the levee and on the deck of the Argosy casino overlooking the swirling brown Mississippi and the refinery and the state capitol and in New Orleans and Gulf Shores and all over the Florida Panhandle. She was eighteen years old.

She had an elongated neck, slender legs, smooth thighs, a calm, somewhat maternal sense, was partial to mysteries, liked art, wanted to study psychology, showed affection to children, old people, stray animals, and despite her many encounters, still viewed the world with compassion and curiosity and kindness.

As much as we were bragging about anything close to sexual conquest in those days, about girls from back home, back in the day, and the supermarket we only *thought* we had a chance with, bragging about how often and how much and how quickly we beat off, even, there came a point when no one could brag on Tammy Z. anymore. She was just now something guys did after getting out of the House, quietly and with compunction, because they could. Later, after what I'm going to tell you about happened, Hymen drilled her in the back bedroom of his ten-wide and then even later, sometime that summer, after she promised everyone things wouldn't be so free and easy anymore, that those days were over and she had no more left to give, Wood convinced her to fall in love with him and then quick-hit her in that same ten-wide and never spoke to her again.

She'd come from nearby Mandeville with one of those hard-to-believe stories—she'd been the prosecution's star witness in a murder trial, her mother the deceased, her father the defendant—that left me feeling both awe and pity when I'd see her around A.A. And then she'd say something—her humble accent missing G's and D's—and lean forward, her fingers grasping unsaid points, for she couldn't speak directly about the case or what happened or the aftermath and her eventual recanting, a recanting which led to an appeal which led to a dismissal which led to freedom and a bank robbery and a dead security guard and her father's eventual lethal injection in Angola, and instead could only talk about how she felt, which was often lonely and confused, as everyone she understood was equally protector and predator, and she'd say something like: It ain't like you think, before leaning back and lifting her short black hair off that straight-edged nape, and dropping one of those Tammy Z. gazes, which always seemed to say, I'm right here, same place I've always been.

And I did know where she was. We all knew. She lived in a three-bedroom apartment off Siegen Lane in South Baton Rouge with four girls who'd just been released from the women's facility—each of them some variation of the usual liar and paper hanger, tweaker, lush, petty whore, thieves, all, needing dual diagnosis, suffering from ADHD, bipolar and hypertension disorder, schizophrenia, borderline, bulimia, and low self-esteem—and whichever guy from the House they were currently screwing.

FOR A WHILE, I struggled with the idea of them—what I wanted, what I didn't want, how it fit with the image I'd constructed of myself at that point in my sobriety. It was, in many ways, the most honest part of my life, and I was happy then, but at eighteen months sober, I pulled a waitress out of a Waffle House on Highway 30 and banged her in Hair-pie's car. All of us got laid. Well. Hair-pie didn't. But everyone else. And you know how that goes—getting wool didn't keep me from wanting more. I was willing to go to any lengths. If you told me they were having a cotton sale in Bayou Boutte, I'd have risked my shitty El Camino dying on the road to check it out. As with most twenty-one-year-old males with all their parts in working order, I was clueless and desperate, in full-on wolf mode, and ignorant.

But then Tammy called the trailer, left a message like Let's kick it. Boom, she said. You're it this week. Want to take me to the Twelve and Twelve?

So there was that—a sure thing!

My sponsor, like so many local old-timers, was *not* impressed.

You're not fucking that girl, he said, please, oh, God, don't fuck her. He leaned over his coffee and cigarette. But if you do, he said, just remember what a drugstore is for.

In those days, he and I talked about everything. Always motives, my deepest and truest reason for my actions. Did I want to buy new underwear and socks because I needed them, or because the gal working the register at Walmart was banging Jim C. and I thought she'd cut me off a slab, too? Was I taking Tammy to the Twelve and Twelve—a barely attended meeting—because I cared about her sobriety, or because I hoped she might slide across the El Camino's bench seats and jack me off? It's impossible to explain my old sponsor's level of service—he was like a father, big brother, zero-interest loan officer, and best friend. He'd become the first person to know exactly who I am and yet trust me in full. I called him daily, often more. He fed me and read the Big Book with me and, in the end, gave me more self-esteem than anything else ever has. He had the patience of Christ. Go on, he said, go on. I know you'll do what's right.

But I told her I'd pick her up at seven-thirty, which was already wrong. The meeting began at eight, and she lived forty minutes away. I showered, gelled my hair, pocketed two packs of cigarettes and twenty dollars spending money, and I brought along a runaway from the woman's facility who was fucking Nob and living with us in the trailers now, a beautiful *maybe*-eighteen-year-old girl.

IN THOSE DAYS, I drove a 1977 El Camino Classic. It had a shift kit, a big engine, the panty-dropping bench seats. I could never keep it on the road. That's the thing about an El Camino. It's like a mustache, nice to look at, twat-bait, sure, but hell to maintain. The gas and oil gauges didn't work. There was no check-engine light. Most days, I had to hammer the starter or cold-wire the ignition just to get it running. And here now, on the way to Baton Rouge, in a corridor of cypress and swamp between the prairie and river in the darkest stretch of I-10 that exists, where, for miles on end, there is nothing but trees, no moon or stars, just darkness, smoke began pouring through the dash.

What is that smell? the runaway asked.

My cigarette, I said, not wanting to alarm her. It was clear the engine had caught fire and would soon lock up. I stepped on the gas and nothing happened.

Throw your cigarette out.

But I didn't want to open my window, afraid the incoming wind might slow us down. I flicked my Zippo at the dash, MPH steadily fell, smoke gushed from the vents.

Am I right? she said.

It's hard to say, I said, though it wasn't. The steering wheel locked up and I coasted into the breakdown lane, where the car died. We got out.

What do you think now? she asked.

Oh, it'll never drive again, I assured her. Shit's toast.

I see, she said.

This girl would one day become a sort of infamous New Orleans stripper, pose nude in magazines, marry well, become a mother and college graduate, but at the time she was still saucy, kind of dirty, and practical: she stuck her maybe-eighteen-year-old thigh out at passing cars while I waited in the darkness.

It didn't take long for some old codger to pull over. He

hopped from his truck, appraising both her and the situation. From the shadows, I could hear this quality to his voice. He really believed she was alone. And then, you know, something shifted, his voice stiffened, when he saw me.

I DON'T REMEMBER what Tammy Z. wore. It wouldn't have mattered. You could've wrapped her body in paper towels and newspaper, padded it with strips of papier-mâché, turned her formless or into an egg, a pear, a fucking donkey, and I still would've been aroused. That's how acute my sense of smell was in those days. We weren't going to any Twelve and Twelve. Hair-pie picked us all up from her place, brought us back to the trailers. He'd memorized an entire season of *The Simpsons* and turned the volume off on the TV and acted out each episode. Read us some of your poetry, man, I begged. Read us that Wordsworth. He donned a satin robe and stood in front of us, reading from a thin volume of poetry. His words were clever, economical, full of grace. They spoke of both the minute and the universal. The night grew incantatory, a feeling crept over us. Tammy's leg kept brushing mine. She twitched every time I lit a smoke.

Hair-pie tried to sit down, but I told him no. Sing us a song, I begged. Sing us something like that Elvis number you did that time before. He was big on show tunes.

But there was something beautiful about Tammy, something sterling and strong, and I knew she wasn't going to sleep with me. Ever.

Leave him alone, she said, placing a protective hand on his thigh.

The runaway shifted her eyes from Tammy Z.'s hand and Hair-pie's thigh to me. She had this look on her face, as if to say, Have you got the message?

It's okay, Hair-pie said.

Go on, I told him, do it.

You're such a dick, Tammy said, and her tone held so much truth.

I'm going to bed, the runaway said pointedly, and so I did, too. Hair-pie was fixing to get laid.

In the morning, I made Hair-pie give me a ride to work. I said, Pony up, bitch. We were halfway to Baker Tanks, out by the river, where I was forming up a slab that would one day be a refueling dock for the big rigs that whistled down Highway 30. I wanted to know what had happened.

Nothing, he said.

His cool enraged me. Ask anyone, I said. Call around. Now. Shoot me straight. What happened?

Nothing, he said.

Say it one more time, I warned. I'll slap you. And I might've— I'd certainly done it before—but he got a tone then.

He shook his head sadly at the road. I'm not sure what you want—

Pull over, I told him. Pull the fuck over. I'm fixing to shit my pants. And I thought I'd punctuate my threat with some flatulence that had been bubbling inside me, but when I held my breath to fart, nothing happened, and so I pushed harder. A turd slid out. Christ, I said. Seriously. Pull over. Hurry.

He jerked to the side of the road and I got out. Beyond the gully on the side of the road was a small patch of wet grass, a clump of trees. I walked into the gully and removed my shorts and underwear. When I got back to Hair-pie's car, he was holding his face very close to the steering wheel.

I'm sorry, he said, if I've disappointed you. I can leave you here if you don't want a ride anymore. I understand.

Don't be crazy, I told him. Of course I want a ride. And I'll need a change of drawers if you have time.

After dropping me off, he drove around awhile, to the call center and then the Gazebo Grill. Neither place offered any ideas. He stopped at the House, where the Silver Fox and Hymen offered similar counsel. After that I guess he drove around a little while longer, stopping at the Circle K for a cappuccino, and then, having forgotten my fresh underwear, went home, crawled in bed with Tammy, and raped her.

Or so we were told, anyway.

WHEN I CAME HOME FROM WORK, the runaway was sitting on the trailer's front steps. I didn't like talking to her much. It was one thing, I figured, to offer refuge to a brother who was clean and doing it. A runaway girl was another matter. No spin would change her function. Normally, Nob and I communicated about everything, but we sidestepped her. For me, this meant ignoring her. It was okay to drive her to Baton Rouge, ostensibly, in a roundabout way, to a meeting, but not okay to talk on that ride. Any other day, I would've shoveled past her without a word, but her shoulders sagged, her hair hung loose about her face. She raised her chin as I approached, and stared bleakly through the pines. All I saw was someone in pain.

I set my tools on the steps and lit a cigarette and looked

beyond the pines at whatever she saw. I asked her where everyone was, but she didn't know, and then I asked if she was okay,
and she said she wasn't, and then I asked if she wanted to talk
about it and she told me the story of what had happened, or
Tammy's version of it, anyway, which was not a good story.
There wasn't much for me to say. I wanted to hug her, but it
seemed inappropriate, so instead I asked who knew. Where
had Tammy gone? Where was Hair-pie? Or the guys?

She began crying. It's your fault, she said. Y'all bully him.

I COULD FEEL MYSELF LOSE CONTROL, telling this story. You
have to imagine. A dinner party. A happy time. Everyone fat
from good food and smart from good conversation. Everyone
sitting around the living room holding their bellies. People
had hot tea, espresso, red wine, digestifs. There was a cheese
board on the coffee table, little plates with mostly eaten cake.
I thought I was telling a story—a ridiculous one, innocent but
not, complicated but simple, absurd, gross, stupid—and yet as
I came to the end, where I contemplated the runaway's words
on the front porch, I looked about the table and saw only
disgust. I can imagine their feelings—How did we get from
your shits and giggles, your tomfoolery, to here? And second,
as someone said: What exactly are you telling us? I was stuck,
and everyone knew it.

What happened? someone asked.

I shook my head.

Was he prosecuted?

Prosecuted, I said, as if I had no idea what the word even
meant.

Yes, they said. *Prosecuted.*

I began retracing the story. Yes, you see, I said, but couldn't finish. All I could think about was the result of this event.

We moved out, I said. We all just moved out. We were so heartbroken by the event that we couldn't even beat Hair-pie's ass. That was our collective imagination. Beating his ass, we decided, had gotten us here. And now it was over for us.

OF COURSE, there's always more to a story, and we did not understand the version of events we'd been presented. No one did. It didn't *seem* like he'd fucked her. It didn't *seem* like there'd been much of anything. We asked Hair-pie again and again for the truth. This was later that night, in some roughshod tribunal organized in our living room. We used diagrams and maps, each adding his own take. It was just the boys now. The runaway had moved on. And later—I'm talking months and years—we'd still be going over this story, still trying to make sense of what exactly had happened, how it had gone down, the exact nature of his assault; I'm talking about kicking gravel in parking lots outside meetings, long after the coffeepot had been emptied and cleaned and the chairs stacked and the floor swept and mopped, and on johnboats in the Atchafalaya and spillway, on endlessly long drives to Grand Isle, legs dangling over a pier, our lines in the water, or sipping DCs and flipping dollar bills at strippers, or in Coffee Call and Waffle House, again and again and again, if only to get it off our chests once more, each time hoping something new might come to light, as new things often do when you tell the same story over and over—someone dies, someone recants—as if we will ever make sense of it, as if there can ever be anything final, until there's no more story to tell, no more facts, no more what really happened, other than what became of us.

Did you fuck her?

He said, I thought she was awake. He said, I thought she was into it.

We said, What do you mean, you *thought she was awake?* Did you *fuck* her?

I asked her, he said.

You said *what?* We were furious.

I said, Are you awake. She seemed like she was in a trance, Hair-pie offered. She was moaning.

Moaning, someone said.

Moaning, he said.

And is that when you did it, you little snake in the grass? Is that when you fucked her?

I, he said. I barely touched her.

He was so sad and regretful that we just sat in silence awhile before Wood said, If you're awake, don't say anything, if you're asleep, say something?

She was in a trance, Hair-pie said again, but so softly you could barely hear him, and he wasn't speaking, after all, to any of us. He was talking to himself. He was telling himself things only he knew.

HERE'S WHAT I DIDN'T SAY at the dinner party: No. I'll tell you what happened. The runaway moved in with Tammy Z. and a girl named P, who I will explain. Nob left town. Hair-pie moved out. Hymen and Wood moved to Baton Rouge near LSU. For a while I drifted, staying first with G-Dub off Chimes and then with P, who I was banging now, and Tammy and the runaway off Siegen in South Baton Rouge. Hymen banged Tammy. Hair-pie moved into an apartment in the same apartment complex off Siegen in South Baton Rouge and came over sometimes and had quiet alone moments with Tammy. There was something friendly in their exchanges. They played with each other as if they were brother and sister, wrestling on the floor or under blankets—never sexual or angry—and I didn't understand it. I still don't—had we lost ourselves over some pawing around? Wood banged Tammy. Hymen began banging the runaway. Me and P moved out, got a town house off Jefferson, still the nicest place I've ever rented. G-Dub began banging Tammy. He moved in with Hymen and Wood. Hair-pie moved a boy into his apartment who stole from him and ran up a five-hundred-dollar phone bill and moved out. He moved another boy into his apartment who stole from him and ran up a five-hundred-dollar phone bill and vandalized his car and moved out. Hymen moved into a place with Hair-pie. The runaway moved in with them. G-Dub moved into an apartment with Tammy. Wood moved into an apartment with an unaffiliated girl. Then it turned out maybe she was affiliated.

We were never together all at once again.

The Eldorado

A few years later, I went to San Francisco to buy a car. On my way back, I visited my dad in Los Angeles. While he was at the doctor, I took a long walk from Beverly Hills to East Hollywood along Sunset Boulevard. This is a part of Los Angeles we think about when we think about the interior parts of the city, though in truth these neighborhoods are very far from the city itself and instead exist only in a showbiz sort of way—stocked with clubs and music venues and ritzy hotels where celebrities stay, it is very much an area where people go to see people and be seen, though I wasn't thinking about any of this on my walk, just running my teeth over the dream a little bit. At some point, I came across a used-car dealership full of classic cars. One of them was a 1970 Cadillac Eldorado, black on black with the knife-edge styling. Something about this car reminded me of being here before, how crazy I'd gotten, how completely insane I'd been, and what it stirred inside me was this feeling of wanting. I had failed before, and I didn't want failure to be the last I knew of this town. I knew what I had to do. Once I returned to Louisiana, I would save up enough money to move out here, and no matter what, I would buy this damn Cadillac.

When I got back to Baton Rouge, I told P I was leaving. She banged some dude from the House. He started calling our apartment. Hello, he'd say, P there?

You should say my name, I'd tell him.

Hey, Tom, he'd say. P there?

Yeah, P is here. Hold on.

I wanted redemption and moved on.

I HAVE MOVED a lot in the years since. Occasionally, like in the winter of 2002 and the summer of 2003, it was because I needed a break from things, some downtime, a chance to clear my head, but for the most part, there was always a better reason. My oldest brother, Aidan, was teaching at a community college in the desert east of L.A., and I moved in with him and his wife so I could attend college. In 2005 Lee moved to San Francisco with his wife and small child, and then Aidan and his wife moved to San Francisco. So I moved to San Francisco, where I finished college. In 2007 I went to grad school in Iowa City. Like I said, there was always a better reason.

In each place I went, I would see these men everywhere. Outside a church or in the park, always clumped, all of them miscast, haggard, paper-thin, struggling to keep a lit match to a snipe, weirdly clean-shaven yet hardscrabble, roughshod but with their shirts tucked in, holes in their faces from piercings and stabbings, they settle on a basketball court even though most have no idea what to do with a ball in their hand, and gather about the one junkie who can actually hoop and try to stop him by any means necessary, yanking his forearm or grabbing his jeans, clotheslining him even as he takes that shit strong to the cup, all the while verbally abusing one another in this perfunctory, loving kind of way. It is always the same bullshit, same slap and tickle, same fuckaround-fuckaround, always the same way they eye me when they catch me listening. Who the fuck are you? Always. Who. The fuck. Are you?

I keep going.

MISS A DIED. The Silver Fox died. P died. Even Program is dead.

We have all moved on.

IF NOTHING ELSE, what I'll say for my dad, after all these years, is that he became one of the world's oldest, longest survivors of AIDS. He keeps going. He doesn't give up. At times, we had a relationship. At times, we were close. At times, he showed me remarkable kindness, and I have had occasion, from time to time, to be there for him. For a while, I carried keys to his apartment, and yet over time, those keys graduated to the glove compartment and then a shoe box and then someone's garage.

Here is the thing about my father: I know all his moves, his indecisions and questions, the doubts he has, his abilities, his confidence within those abilities. I know his knee gets cranky after long drives. A knot bulges from his lower back some days. He gets headaches if he doesn't sleep well. And I know about his relationships—his initial hopes, the indignities he feels, his eventual impatience, rigidity; everything is beautiful, when new. I know him. And he knows me. Not much I could say or do would surprise him. We have the same feet, same hands, same tension in our neck and temples. We are both tall, funny at times, and not bad looking. We are paranoid, private, guarded. Both of us employ candor as a shield, or stories. We are competitive. We eat a lot. We both feel alone, and enjoy being alone, and yet we both need people. I love him. I always want to reach out and hug him. But he has not been my dad all these years. And that's okay. At some point, I gave up all my expectations for who and what he'd be in my life. But years passed, a decade or two, and I came to understand I could not stop expecting. Another way of saying it: forgiveness doesn't always happen just because you want to forgive. It doesn't occur in one sitting. There's always another hill, another hole. It's a continual process. There have been many highs and lows, a lot of awful. Many times, I've looked at him and wondered, truly wondered, why I want him in my life at all.

I've ridden out most of these years looking for someone else with whom I could never fully own the awful. I've engaged in some risky behavior. I've gone to some unfamiliar yet familiar place, a part of town or a house, each one of them dangerous, avoidable, a place I shouldn't have been, each time believing what I'd find would be important somehow.

Have I wanted to die? I don't know. If yes, then my question is why haven't I, and if I say no, then my question is why behave this way?

I went from Iowa City to Los Angeles to San Francisco—women, different—but then got offered an apartment on Cape Cod and a sum of money to write whatever the hell I wanted to write, and so I moved out there. From Cape Cod I went to Baltimore. I was broke. It seemed like a good place. Then I met a girl who was moving to San Francisco and tagged along, but we broke up as well. To sum it up—in the years since I left the House, it has gone something like this: Louisiana, Los Angeles, Louisiana, Los Angeles, Riverside, Los Angeles, Riverside, San Francisco, Iowa City, Los Angeles, San Francisco, Provincetown, Baltimore, San Francisco, and so on. In other words, let's bang each other and go, bang each other and go, bang and go, until we are all gone from each other.

I never bought the Eldorado.

AND YET THIS: years and years later, I moved back to Los Angeles again. This was going to be it, I promised myself. No more moving, no more bullshit. I was thirty-eight, my dad was still alive—he'll probably outlive me—though we'd grown distant, and I didn't tell him that I'd moved back, nor that I lived a few blocks from his apartment, and I didn't plan to. He wasn't the reason I'd come back, at least that's what I told myself. I just wanted to be somewhere warm when I died. I'd had some cancer scares of late.

All the same, I thought about him, and many, many nights, I found myself taking lonely childhood-haunted strolls in the vicinity of his building. Always furtive, encased in shadows, I'd creep down his block, peek inside his garage, and, if his car was gone, climb the trellis to his balcony, where I could peer inside his living room and kitchen. The dust of Los Angeles coated his balcony, a flaking of desert and smog and skin. Bachelor droppings littered his place: dirty dishes towered from the sink, coffee grounds coated the floor, trash cans overflowed, on the floor were dirty socks, old receipts, balled paper towels, and crumpled pants.

It looked a lot like my own place.

One day, I was walking to the doctor feeling shitty about things, morose, even, sentimental, thinking it would all be over soon, that I'd die, poor me, and was passing this middle school in the afternoon, watching children scream across the playground, my mind unraveling, remembering my mom's warm eyes, Abba running his hands through my hair, Lee smiling, Lee's kid, Aidan's kids, how I had no kids and no hope of them, really, and in that lack of hope, no place of my own to come back to, and no home—it had been thirteen years since I'd been to Louisiana, two decades since I'd been to Georgia, and who would have wanted to have kids with me in these years?

I began that pre-cry thing, a heaviness behind my eyes, blubbering a little, then sobbing, sobbing like I hadn't in years, and in this sobbing I squinted—I can't make this up—at the playground and saw beyond the kids, next to a bench, two grown men talking, one of them very old and with his hands in his pockets, and I didn't think anything other than Huh, that's familiar somehow, and kept walking, but then—and here's where it gets weird—from the corner of my eye, I noticed the old man gesturing with his fingers as he made one point after another: it was my dad.

I kept walking.

And was it that night or later that week or months later when I saw a girl standing on the corner of Figueroa and Eighth, holding her purse in both hands, offering a slight redistribution of weight from one hip to the other as I approached?

Her mouth spread, her eyes lit up. Even my shortcomings were charming. You've failed a little, her smile said, so what?

Her name was Kristen, and in short order we went to Palm Springs, Petaluma, Santa Barbara, Joshua Tree, and the Salton

Sea. Here was a place I'd been many times before, though never long enough to stay the night and look at the defunct hole in the middle of another hole, a very big hole, so deep and far and wide, and see it for it was. We could barely make out the train on the opposite side of the water, even as it began to spread, its tail emerging from rocks, this sudden swath of dust getting wider and wider until it was something else completely. And I told her things. But for the first time, I believed them. I could see slight changes in the smallest things: I wore collared shirts even when she said I didn't have to. It didn't matter whether I was clean or dirty—I had to wear my collared shirt as long as possible, so she'd see it and know what I meant in wearing it. I wore a tie some days. Same thing. Kept it on long after my intention was known. Act as if, was what they'd said. Such was the force of my feelings for her that I needed her to meet my dad, needed her to know where I'd come from, and I needed him to meet her; I wanted him in my life. For his part, he has obliged—I still get a little shot of self-worth every time he calls.

As for my mom and Abba and me, we laugh about a lot of these things now.

It didn't surprise me when I got offered another residency, three thousand–plus miles away. For a few days, I imagined being alone, old habits, that terminal velocity, staggering dumb, helter-skelter, rinse-repeat, rinse-repeat, over and over until all my hair has come out and my teeth are gone, before realizing something about Kristen was different and, more important, something in me with her.

So we packed our places. Of course, hers took way, way longer than mine. She'd lived in her apartment a long time. Her calendars had yellowed, her pantry was full, even her mice had grown old and passed on. This was a place of spiders who'd lived out their natural lives watching their offspring carry on. Families of raccoons lived here. Flocks of parrots. Late at night, coyotes would come from the hills or arroyo and stalk the backyards and cul-de-sacs, always searching for water or some small animal to eat, and yet there can be a decency to even the coldest of predators, and many of the squirrels were old. She'd lived here so long she'd seen them all, generation after generation, knew each of their offspring's names.

On our way, she said, I want you to show me where you come from.

It took me all the way to Abilene, roughly two thousand miles into what stretched to a four-thousand-mile trip, before I made the phone call.

HAIR-PIE SAYS, Sure, we'd love to have y'all. He's married now. He and his husband have just built a large home near the river. They are successful but, more important, happy. They have a wonderful home. His husband makes up a welcome basket. They cook dinner for us, a glorious dinner.

We plan to visit the House, and I call the few numbers left in my phone, get bad news. The House has been destroyed in the recent flood, and all the brothers have been moved out. We drive up and down West Road. I am looking for the crack houses and crack whores, but there are just houses now, regular houses, piled on top of one another, one house after another. The fields are gone, replaced by subdivisions. The old tin-sided liquor store is gone. Even the gully we used to clean has changed—culverts have been dropped in and covered in concrete.

All that's left of the group room is the Big Board.

That night, sitting on Hair-pie's screened-in porch, Kristen listens to us go over some of the stories. Some of them I've told already. Others I've forgotten. Like that time what's-his-face peed on the group room floor. Or when I tried to jump a bayou in my El Camino. What a dumbass, I say. Like it was the goddamn General Lee. I'm smoking, we are all laughing. We go over most of them. Hair-pie reminds me of a guy who came to our trailer looking for me. He was a debt collector, but instead of a suit and tie, he wore a .38 tucked into his jeans and a skinning knife in his boot. He knocked on the door and, when Hair-pie opened it, asked if Tom was around. Hair-pie didn't even hesitate. Sure, he said. Come right in.

I get it, I say. It's funny.

Hair-pie laughs. Fuck you.

Kristen looks from him to me and then back to him. I hadn't heard that one.

No? Hair-pie says. There are others.

I've heard a lot, she says.

I'm sure you have.

I thought he was lying, she says.

Naw, Hair-pie says, they're all true.

All of them? she asks, though there's no point she's making here other than an illumination of her surprise.

All of them, he says.

He is not menacing. Neither am I. We are both just old.

You boys are so disgusting, she says, though I know she loves me.

Later, after she excuses herself for the night, Hair-pie and I remain on the porch.

For a long while we sit there. So long the ashtray overflows. So long I stand and stretch. So long I pull my chair to the door, where I flick my cigarette butts onto his manicured lawn. One by one, as the night wears on, I watch lights go out in neighboring windows up and down the road. We are telling each other stories. The same ones we've told again and again. On porches. After a meal. Or in phone calls. Or on fishing trips. On long rides in the days when we still rode together. They aren't all good stories, nor do they highlight the goodness in me, or in the men like him whom I once called my brothers, for we each possess this thing inside us at once horrible and beautiful, shocking yet predictable, known and familiar, unavoidable, tragic, easily explainable, infinite, finite, ridiculous, absurd, all-pervading, redundant, garden-variety and unusual, the same, dissimilar, surprising, smart, terrifying, and dumb, each one of us lucky, unlucky, blessed, bewitched, and doomed. Each begins the same and each one ends the same. We are rabid and hell-bent, maniacal, desperate.

Somewhere in the night, I feel a breeze come up over the delta off the Gulf; soft and barely lifting my shirt, it cools the sweat upon my nape—I hear crickets, bullfrogs, and we keep telling each other these stories.

It's the one place I've ever felt at home.

Acknowledgments

Too many people have helped me with this book to thank here. You have offered me time, a room, a roof, money, food, a phone or computer, a tie, a razor, an ear, support, hope, kindness, and love. You have given me rides, bought me a bus pass, or lent me your car. And you have believed in me when I was unbelievable and no one else would. Or you have offered only indifference. I am grateful for all.

About the Author

Tom Macher grew up mostly in Georgia and spent his teenage years bouncing between California and New York, Montana and Louisiana, living in boys' homes, halfway houses, and communes. He is a graduate of the University of Iowa Writers' Workshop and a former fiction fellow at the Fine Arts Work Center in Provincetown. *Halfway* is his first book.